CORBA Developer's Guide with XML

George M. Doss

Wordware Publishing, Inc.

Library of Congress Cataloging-in-Publication Data

Doss, George M.
  CORBA developer's guide with XML / by George M. Doss.
    p. cm.
  Includes index.
  ISBN 1-55622-668-3 (pbk.)
  1. XML (Document markup language).   2. CORBA (Computer architecture).
  I. Title.
  QA76.76.H94D68   1999
  005.7'2--dc21   99-22029
                                                      CIP

ISBN 1-55622-668-3
10 9 8 7 6 5 4 3 2 1
9907

Product names mentioned are used for identification purposes only and may be trademarks of their respective companies.

All inquiries for volume purchases of this book should be addressed to Wordware Publishing, Inc., at the above address. Telephone inquiries may be made by calling:

(972) 423-0090

Dedication

This book is dedicated to all my teachers—good or bad, remembered or forgotten, formal or informal. They all contributed to what I know today.

Acknowledgements

This is my fourth book with Wordware Publishing, Inc. I would again like to thank the fine people who seek to make the writing process more fun and easier than it should be. I would like to thank several people. Jim Hill, publisher, had the fortitude to ask me to write another book on CORBA. Beth Kohler and Kellie Key, editors, made the words that I set down clearer and more readable. Denise McEvoy, interior designer, makes bland manuscripts look professional. Alan McCuller, cover designer, showed once again his magic in designing an eye-catching cover. And finally, Pamela Alba, executive assistant, and her friendly smile that got me through the administrative hurdles.

I would like to thank especially all those people who contributed to the source documentation on CORBA and XML.

Any omissions or technical misinterpretations are mine.

George M. Doss

Plano, TX

Contents Summary

Contents

Part I—XML: Why and What

Introduction

Web or Internet technologies, especially those that can be labeled object-oriented, are in flux. This book associates two of these technologies: Extensible Markup Language (XML) and Common Object Request Broker Architecture (CORBA). This book makes brief references to Java, an object-oriented, controlling programming language, as a kind of cement or glue. This book also discusses Standard Generalized Markup Language (SGML) because XML and Hypertext Markup Language (HTML) are both children of this programming language.

While the first design goal of the XML Recommendation states "XML shall be straightforwardly usable over the Internet"[1] it can be demonstrated that XML has broad application in such areas as e-commerce. With this in mind, this book focuses on XML document type definitions (DTD) design using the structures of CORBA so one might get a new perspective on programming in an object-oriented environment. It is not a book that teaches XML, but rather discusses design for experienced object-oriented developers. One needs to comprehend how an analysis of an environment, CORBA, assists in design and development of XML elements, attributes, and entities that reflect that environment.

CORBA documentation is extensive. The contributors to CORBA development all seek four core design goals—interoperability, portability, scalability, and reusability. One can analyze CORBA documentation from many views. The one used in this book is to analyze some of the variables in different interface sets (CORBAservices, CORBAfacilities, and domains) to see how one could model XML document structures. The analysis does not actually consider values, but how an XML document has potential for integration of local network data with various CORBA interfaces.

---

[1]   Extensible Markup Language (XML) 1.0 W3C Recommendation 10-February-1998; URL is
      http://www.w3.org/TR/1998/REC-xml-19980210.

Note: This book discusses design and development processes, not the actual how-to-do-this. There are many vendors available to assist in unique local CORBA integration issues.

For one to use the full power of XML, one must create one's own XML document type definition (DTD). One then takes a most critical step by establishing a document's grammar (the implicit rules) and its unique <u>meaningful</u> markup. This follows to a certain degree precedence, designing DTDs for XML dialects such as Chemical Markup Language (CML).

XML enables generic SGML to serve, receive, and process in the same way as HTML does on the Web. This means XML can describe a document and can establish hyperlinks as HTML. It is also a bit more. XML handles data in a document. XML gives one the capability to manipulate (manage or handle) data from a document into a database and vice versa.

XML also extends (1) HTML's capabilities to handle document control, (2) the function to publish information in a variety of media from the same source, (3) the ability to establish complex documentation links, and (4) the design technique for defining different document descriptions. These notions are found in XML's name, extensible.

CORBA is a standard for defining a network as object-oriented in comparison to client/server. A basic premise of object-oriented (OO) theory is that a client can access or can be accessed. The same holds true for a server. CORBA can define these objects in two major areas: CORBAservices (see Chapter 8) and CORBAfacilities (see Chapter 9).

Java is an object-oriented language designed to be:

- Reusable
- Portable
- Interoperable

Besides these three, there are seven other Java characteristics that are important as a part of justification for moving to Java internetworking:

- Application adaptation is possible because of dynamic network downloading.
- Application performance is increased.
- Design, development, testing, and implementation are simpler because of component-level object programming.
- Development time is shorter because of code reuse.

- Memory management increases system robustness.
- Multithreading produces high performance in GUI functions.
- Security is improved because the Java run-time system checks for viruses.

SGML became a global text-processing standard in 1986 through the International Organization for Standardization (ISO).[2] It became a standard through the hard work of many, but in particular Charles F. Goldfarb. SGML is the parent of XML. XML extends SGML's document paradigm to the hypertext environment of the Internet (see Chapters 1 and 2). The name of the standard is "ISO 8879: 1986 Information processing—Text and Office systems—Standard Generalized Markup Language (SGML)."

Note: Before SGML there were Script and GML (Generalized Markup Language). Charles F. Goldfarb, Ed Mosher, and Ray Lorie at IBM developed the idea to enable document sharing among different IBM systems. XML is like most Internet technologies in that its origin extends back a number of decades.

Probably the most precise way to define HTML is a method, a markup language, which describes an electronic page that uses links (hypertext) to associate a series of such pages that become an electronic document. One could say "In the beginning (a British overstatement) was HTML and it was found wanting." Actually, there was manuscript (writing by hand), the printed document that looked like a manuscript (check out the Gutenberg Bible as originally printed), and more variations on this theme until the computer environment. The computer environment has or had Script, Generalized Markup Language (GML), Standard Generalized Markup Language (SGML), Hypertext Markup Language (HTML), and Extensible Markup Language (XML). This is a poor man's history of publishing in less than 50 words. Left out are key items such as pictographs (wall paintings), cuneiform (wedge-shaped writing), hieroglyphics (sound symbolic writing), ideograms (idea symbolic writing), and Virtual Reality Markup Language (VRML).

---

2   The group in French is known as *Organisation Internationale de Normalisation.* ISO is not the group's acronym, but comes from the Greek "isos" meaning "equal."

Book's Audience

This book is for system administrators, MIS managers, and network designers and developers that want to or have been tasked to use the latest Web technologies, in particular CORBA and XML, to enhance their system. Any system enhancement involves ever-changing goals, issues, and techniques that include:

- System architecture and configuration
- Operating systems
- Protocols
- Management tools
- Application software
- Graphical user interfaces (browsers)
- User activities, abilities, and needs

Because of the above situation, this book considers selected processes for solving some of these issues. The methodologies given here enable you, the system administrator, to evaluate effectively and efficiently how XML design can be used in CORBA networking. Also, one must consider the relationships among XML, SGML, HTML, and Java to achieve a more comprehensive user-friendly environment.

This book is also for people who assist the system administrator either in policy or design integration. This would include:

- Design and development team
- Product vendors
- Consultants
- Support technicians
- Documentation and training groups
- Users (internal, customers, or vendors)

This book is for anyone who has tried to read Extensible Markup Language (XML) 1.0, W3C Recommendation (10 February 1998). The Recommendation is the result of lengthy discussions by experts in publishing technology. The experts were trying to resolve how to use the best design considerations of two worlds, SGML and HTML. One of their goals was to write a concise statement of the results of the discussions. The Recommendation is a set of 89 production rules with minimal commentary.

There are no alternatives given. There are no how-we-got-there statements.

Their concern was and is data and text structure, not appearance.

Finally, this book is for anyone who has tried to read the extensive CORBA documentation available. When any new network architecture is developed, one should expect technical clarifications. This book tries to give a twisted view of reality for the developer who is challenged by the weight of documentation. A "simple" view of CORBA is that it is "a set of interfaces" and "its variables" are the keys to comprehension.

Key Issues

The first issue is that the XML Recommendation was only completed in February 1998 after a 15-month effort. This area is dynamic to say the least. There are already ideas on the table to extend XML with such things as Extensible Stylesheet Language (XSL). There are also legacy hardware and software issues. There are such things as lack of tools (parsers) and experience. Because one knows or had experiences with SGML or HTML does not make one an expert with XML. There are only 89 XML production rules, but this book tries to demonstrate that there are many nuances to each rule. There are least 500 permutations for all the rules.

 Note: A goal of the W3C XML Activity was to have a concise document. The document is approximately 30 pages. It has minimal commentary.

The second issue is that the CORBA documentation is as extensive as XML documentation is sparse. There are multiple committees working on special facets of the infrastructure for CORBAservices, CORBAfacilities, and domains. There is the expectation that a new version of the general specification will be released in 1999.

Focus Is

This book focuses on a process for designing XML document type definitions (DTDs) in the context of the CORBA infrastructure. It is a design guide to assist developers who need to work with CORBA by demonstrating the importance of CORBA interface variables as viewed through an XML DTD design process. Also the book is concerned with languages that can assist in defining or modeling CORBA objects and can also assist in the design and development of XML DTDs for CORBA.

This book uses different metaphors to try to highlight "sound bites" of information on CORBA. Two metaphors used are "news headlines" and "document."

Focus Is-Not

This book is <u>not</u> a comprehensive answer to integrating XML into CORBA. It is <u>not</u> a programming guide such as one for Java. It is <u>not</u> an XML markup guide per se since the focus is only on the first and most critical step in XML design—the development of XML DTDs. And finally, the book is <u>not</u> an explanation of CORBA interworkings.

Each system administrator or developer must consider other factors such as legacy hardware, legacy software, system configurations, and users. Also, skill sets, project goals, and customer goals have to be considered.

Expectations about the Readers

So there are no surprises as to what is not in this book, here is a list of expectations about the reader:

- Reader has a system-level knowledge of the technologies (protocols, servers) of the Internet and of an intranet.
- Introducing CORBA into a system is a goal of the reader's corporation and he or she wants to determine the potentials of XML as a part of the system's design.
- Reader is a key player in the development of the network either as the system administrator or in another technical role. However, other types of readers (marketing, training, documentation, and general management) may be interested in concepts developed in this book.
- Reader has a basic awareness of what takes place when new applications are introduced in a system.
- Reader has a basic knowledge of the jargon of computer science.
- Reader's system has a configuration different from any other.
- Reader can draw upon internal and external technical resources.

Basic Position of the Author

Here are the basic notions that underlie this book:

■ There is no one way to design or develop XML DTDs, but there are rules for these activities.

■ No one person can effectively design and develop all the XML DTDs for a system in a short time.

■ Creating XML DTDs is a logical evolutionary process.

■ The reader should use the technical expertise of vendors, not their marketing expertise.

■ The end goals for CORBA and XML are the same as the reasons for using Java: interoperability, portability, and reusability.

■ It is necessary to get a definition of customer expectations for

❑ Why they want to use CORBA.

❑ When they are going to use them.

❑ Where they are going to use them.

❑ What they want in them.

❑ How they are going to be used.

■ It is necessary to explain to the customers what part of their expectations is achievable based on

❑ Budgetary restrictions

❑ Technological developments

❑ Time limitations

Significance of CORBA 3.0

The Object Management Group (Framingham, MA) has scheduled CORBA 3.0 for release by the end of 1999. This version of CORBA simplifies the use of CORBA ORBs for the development of distributed object applications. New features include:

■ Enhanced Java language to IDL mapping

■ Improved quality of service features

❑ Embedded environment support

❑ Real-time CORBA 1.0

■ New messaging support

■ Support for distributed components

❑ Component Model

❏ CORBA Scripting Language
❏ Multiple interfaces
❏ Objects-by-value
■ Support for legacy environments
❏ DCE/CORBA interworking
❏ Firewalls

Note: The design process is not limited because of an impending new release except for the consideration of new interfaces and variables. Any design process should acknowledge the need for scalability since one can expect a CORBA 4.0.

Enhanced Java Language to IDL Mapping

The new Java language to IDL mapping specification allows developers to build distributed applications completely in Java and then generates the CORBA IDL from the Java class files. This allows other binary applications to access Java applications using Remote Method Invocation (RMI) over Internet Inter-ORB Protocol (IIOP). For details on the Java side, see JDK 1.2 documents and in particular information on the idltojava compiler.

Improved Quality of Service Features

This specification defines improved service with minimal CORBA addresses required for a CORBA-compliant system that can operate in an embedded environment. This opens the door for the use of CORBA in embedded devices.

For developers to have more direct control over ORB resource allocation, a new type of ORB called the Real-time ORB has also been specified. Such an ORB might be comprised of fixed priority scheduling, control over ORB resources for end-to-end predictability, and flexible communications. Real-time CORBA should be useful for time-critical and process control applications.

New Messaging Support

The Asynchronous Messaging specification has two components: levels of quality of service (QoS) agreements and Interface Definition Language (IDL) changes necessary to support asynchronous method invocations.

This enhances CORBA abilities to support synchronous, deferred synchronous, and one-way messaging. QoS policies tell the ORB how to handle various delivery scenarios.

Support for Distributed Components

The new CORBA Component Model specifies a framework for the development of "plug-and-play" CORBA objects. The model encapsulates the creation, life cycle, and events for a single object and allows clients to explore dynamically an object's capabilities, methods, and events.

The ability to have multiple interfaces allows a single object to present multiple views of itself through an interface selection mechanism. This ability allows a program access to an object's functions based on interface definitions, operations, or other criteria.

CORBA 3.0 assists programmers using objects-by-value to integrate CORBA more seamlessly into object-oriented programming languages such as Java. Objects-by-value are passed as parameters rather than as references.

The new CORBA Scripting Language specification removes memory allocation and deallocation, memory pointers, and compilation and linking procedures. One can compose CORBA components into applications. It allows client developers to create and access CORBA servers, while focusing on integration for the development of business logic.

Support for Legacy Environments

CORBA 3.0 can assist programmers in their legacy environments, particularly:

- Firewalls
- DCE application integration

The CORBA 3.0 Firewall specification defines interfaces for passing IIOP through a firewall. The options allow the firewall to have filters and proxies on either side. This specification extends the secure use of CORBA to the Internet and across organizational boundaries.

The DCE/CORBA Interworking specification provides a roadmap for integrating legacy DCE applications into CORBA environments. There are new options for ensuring extended use of legacy applications.

Key Questions

Here are just a few of the questions that should have some resolution by the last page of the book:

- What is an XML application? Is there more than one type?
- What is a CORBAservice?
- What is a CORBAfacility?
- How does XML relate to SGML?
- How does XML compare to HTML?
- How does one use Java in developing an XML application?
- What is a process for designing and developing an XML application?

Book Outline

Part I—XML: Why and What

Chapter 1—Foundational View

This chapter briefly looks at the practical implications of XML and considers these areas:

- Background information
- XML grammar overview
- XML benefits
- XML and SGML comparison
- XML and HTML comparison
- XML and Java comparison

Chapter 2—XML Design Policy

This chapter heavily uses the language of the XML Recommendation 1.0 (10 February 1998) to give a foundational basis for further discussions on how to implement production. The place and order of a production rule is important in an implementing context. This chapter gives an overview of the Recommendation and discusses:

- Production rules overview
- Well-formed documents
- Valid documents

- Logical structures
- Physical structures
- XML processor constraints

 Warning: One should always refer to the latest version of the Extensible Markup Language Recommendation.[3] The Recommendation, not this book, should be the ultimate document on XML.

Chapter 3—Developing an XML Document Type Definition (DTD)

This chapter includes three parts:

First, this chapter gives ten frequently asked questions about a DTD. The answers to these questions are expanded upon in various sections of this chapter.

Second, this chapter looks at the fundamental process for developing a document type definition (DTD). The ideas given are extended in the chapters on developing DTDs for CORBAservices and CORBAfacilities.

Third, this chapter also includes discussions on some key tools for developing a DTD and XML documents. Three of the tools discussed are parsers, editors, and browsers.

Chapter 4—Document Object Model Overview

This chapter reviews one of the latest technologies that is related to XML: the Document Object Model (DOM). The focus is on the DOM Specification Level 1 (1 October 1998). The DOM permits one to view an XML document as a data holder and as an object of the CORBA paradigm. The DOM should be the API standard for handling XML documents in applications, browsers, and editors. Included at the end of the chapter is a four-part example of Java code, an XML DTD, XML markup, and DOM output.

---

3   The latest Recommendation version can be found starting with the URL http://www.w3.org/TR.

Chapter 5—DCAM, IDL, and UML Overviews

This chapter discusses three developing Web technologies and their implications for developing XML applications for CORBA. A part of the Distributed Component Architecture Modeling (DCAM) effort is to develop taxonomies into standard format for such products as browsers, IDLs, Web tools and servers, message brokers (CORBA, COM+, etc.), and application frameworks. The Interface Definition Language (IDL) describes CORBA objects. The Unified Modeling Language is used in developing models of CORBA objects and infrastructure.

Chapter 6—Web Interface Definition Language (WIDL)

This chapter overviews the Web Interface Definition Language (WIDL), an important new Web technology for conceptual developing of XML applications for CORBA from webMethods. This technology goes hand-in-hand with the Document Object Model (DOM) and Distributed Component Architecture Modeling (DCAM) technologies.

This chapter considers four key notions about WIDL:

- WIDL overview
- WIDL-SPEC DTD
- WIDL-MAPPING DTD
- WIDL implications for XML and CORBA

Part II—CORBA: Why and What

Chapter 7—CORBA Headlines

This chapter uses the "news headline" metaphor as a method for searching for the components, features, functions, or parts of CORBA that can be equated to XML elements, attributes, or entities. The search includes a look at the architecture, the ORB, domains, CORBAservices, Security Service, and CORBAfacilities. The chapter ends with a very basic designed XML/CORBA DTD.

Chapter 8—Essentials of CORBAservices

This chapter briefly establishes essentials of descriptive information of CORBAservices for the development of a document type definition (DTD) for a document type labeled *services* (Chapter 12). A Security Service DTD is developed in Chapter 13 with a document type labeled *security*, and more details are given there.

Chapter 9—Essentials of CORBAfacilities

As with the discussion on CORBAservices in Chapter 8, this chapter focuses CORBAfacilities architecture or infrastructure, rather than the "how-to," for the purpose of gaining information for designing an XML document type definition (DTD) for CORBAfacilities in Chapter 14. The information given here is based on OMG's document for CORBAfacilities, version 4.0 (November 1995).

Part III—XML Applications

Chapter 10—Design and Development Issues

This chapter outlines ten general key design and development issues. Besides the general principles one needs to clarify specific issues. These issues come in two categories, single environment or multiple environments. A single environment could consist of CORBA itself. A multiple environment would consist of both CORBA and XML integration. This chapter discusses both categories for CORBA, XML, HTML, and Java.

Chapter 11—Designing an XML DTD for CORBA Domains

This chapter reflects on the design issues for developing XML DTDs for CORBA domains at a very high level. This chapter also briefly looks at the potential of CORBA domains and the potential use of XML with various domains through discussions about seven interoperability issues.

Chapter 12—Designing an XML DTD for CORBAservices

This chapter discusses the planning, designing, and developing of an XML DTD for CORBAservices based on information from Chapter 8 and the CORBAservices Specification (various chapters are dated 1996-1997). The premise here is that an XML document can handle data and that CORBA is fundamentally a series of interfaces; thus, one can design an XML document that organizes and declares the variables that might go into the interfaces.

The document type definition (DTD) for CORBAservices is broadly structured using the interfaces for declaring XML elements. The information given here is a high-level model for looking at the issue of CORBA/XML integration. It is recognized that an object-oriented programming language such as Java would be required to complete this integration.

Chapter 13—Designing an XML DTD for the Security Service

This chapter discusses some issues for design and development of an XML DTD that reflects key security functionality and CORBA implementation of a Security service. One must be knowledgeable of two items:

- Fundamental security attributes
- CORBA security service interfaces

The interfaces are suited for three types of people:

- Administrator
- Application developer
- Implementor

This chapter closes with guidelines for designing a "DTD system" for a CORBA security service. Local factors determine an actual model.

Chapter 14—Designing an XML DTD for CORBAfacilities

This chapter describes some XML elements and attribute lists for some of the twelve facilities that make up CORBAfacilities based on information from Chapter 9 and the CORBAfacilities: Common Facilities Architecture V4.0 November 1995 Specification. The premise here is that an XML document can handle data and that one uses the concepts developed for CORBAfacilities as a starting point for eventual CORBA/XML integration. This chapter is basically a "what-if" rather than a "how-to" chapter.

Chapter 15—Final Thoughts, Summary, and Conclusions

This chapter looks at the future possibilities of the ideas discussed in prior chapters. There is a summary of the key ideas present in the prior chapters. There are some high level general conclusions on XML document type definitions based on a CORBA framework.

Part IV—Appendixes

Appendix A—Terms and Definitions

This appendix defines key CORBA and XML terms used in this book.

Appendix B—XML Alphabetical Production Rules List

This appendix lists in alphabetical order 89 products and their associated production rule numbers from XML Working Recommendation 1.0 (10 February 1998). See also Appendix C.

Appendix C—XML Production Rules

This appendix summarizes the XML production rules from XML Working Recommendation 1.0 (10 February 1998). See also Appendix B and Appendix D.

Appendix D—Constraints

This appendix summarizes the well-formedness and validity constraints from XML Working Recommendation 1.0 (10 February 1998). These constraints are required for designing a conforming XML processor. See also Appendix C.

Appendix E—XML Web Sites

This appendix gives key XML Web sites for getting the latest information on subjects discussed in this book.

Appendix F—XML Markup Examples

This appendix shows some very simple examples of generalized XML markup.

Book Navigation

The book may be read from cover or cover or used as a reference book. The table of contents or index may direct you to points of interest since you may already have a specific solution.

Companion CD-ROM

The companion CD-ROM contains a multimedia presentation to explain the essential concepts of the XML Specification, along with a trial version of XML Authority from Extensibility, Inc. Please see the last page of the book and the CD itself for more information.

Part I

XML: Why and What

Included in This Part:

- Chapter 1—Foundational View

- Chapter 2—XML Design Policy

- Chapter 3—Developing an XML Document Type
  Definition (DTD)

- Chapter 4—Document Object Model Overview

- Chapter 5—DCAM, IDL, and UML Overviews

- Chapter 6—Web Interface Definition Language
  (WIDL)

Chapter 1

Foundational View

Included in This Chapter:

- ❏ Background Information
- ❏ XML Grammar Overview
- ❏ XML Benefits
- ❏ XML and SGML Comparison
- ❏ XML and HTML Comparison
- ❏ XML and Java Comparison

This chapter looks at Extensible Markup Language (XML) in descriptive, it-is-this, terms rather than in prescriptive, how-to-use, terms. Chapter 2 discusses the theoretical underpinnings, the production rules, based on XML Recommendation 1.0 (10 February 1998).

Note: As of the writing of this book, the Recommendation lacks final approval as a Standard. The authors expect minimal changes to the Recommendation.

XML is a subset of SGML with the powers of HTML. With XML one can speak of a Web-based document rather than of a Web-based page as with HTML.

This chapter looks at very briefly:

■ XML's background

■ XML's grammar

■ XML's benefits

■ XML and SGML comparison

■ XML and HTML comparison

■ XML and Java comparison

Note: Later chapters discuss in detail many of the specialized uses of words in this chapter. Also see Appendix A, "Terms and Definitions."

Background Information

XML's actual history is very brief since the first working draft was published in November 1996. XML's foundation comes from the Standard Generalized Markup Language (SGML) that was published in 1986 as ISO 8879 (1986 Information processing—Text and Office systems—Standard Generalized Markup Language (SGML)). The reality of SGML as a standard for electronic documentation markup comes through the dedicated efforts of Charles F. Goldfarb.

The W3C XML Activity, a working group of the World Wide Web Consortium (W3C), developed XML. The editors were Tim Bray, Jean Paoli, and C.M. Sperberg-McQueen.

XML Recommendation 1.0 shows precisely how XML design eases implementation and SGML and HTML interoperability. If one takes time to read the Recommendation, not an easy task, look for all sentences that begin "For interoperability...." The Recommendation (Specification) is a very short document and is very precise. One should read the Recommendation in HTML format so one can follow the links.

Note: This book includes a computer-based training (CBT) course that summarizes the key ideas of the Recommendation. The CBT's structural design primarily uses the Recommendation document structure including numbered sub-sections.

XML Grammar Overview

The key to comprehending the XML production rules is to know the notation rules or grammar. There are two views of XML grammar: the Extended Backus-Naur Form (EBNF) notation and the language developed in the Recommendation. EBNF was used to define the XML production rules. The rules defined the formal grammar of XML. A production rule takes this form:

```
Symbol ::= expression
```

The Recommendation uses 16 right-hand EBNF rules. One uses these rules as a basis for the construction of production rules.

1. #xN

   N is a hexadecimal integer.

   Expression matches the character in ISO/IEC 10646 whose canonical (UCS-4) code value, when interpreted as an unsigned binary number, has the value indicated.

   For further details, see ISO/IEC 10646-1993 (E). Information technology—Universal Multiple-Octet Coded Character Set (UCS)—Part I: Architecture and Basic Multilingual Plane. [Geneva]: ISO, 1993 (plus amendments AM 1 through AM 7). The Web site is either:

   http://charts.unicode.org/ or **ftp.unicode.org/Public/2.1-Update**

   Example:

   White space (Production Rule 3) equals one of the following in the format of #xN:

   #x20—space
   #x9—horizontal tab
   #xD—carriage return
   #xA—line feed

2. [a-zA-Z],[#xN-#xN]

Matches any character within the defined range(s).

The ISO/IEC 10646 defines a character as a specified unit, such as a tab, Latin A, Latin a, etc.

See also the Unicode Standard, located at **http://charts.unicode.org**.

Example:

Character range in Production Rule 2 is defined as:

```
Char ::= #x9 | #xA | #xD | [#x20-#xD7FF] | [#xE000-#xFFFD] |
[#x10000-#x10FFFF]
```

See also the Unicode Standard.

3. [^a-z],[^#xN-xN]

Matches any character outside the defined range(s). The character ^ represents "not."

The ISO/IEC 10646 defines a character as a specified unit, such as a tab, Latin A, etc.

See also the Unicode Standard.

Example:

The general declarations of XML do not use this notation.

Production Rule 14 for character data states:

```
CharData ::= [^<&]* - ( [^<&]* ']]>' [^<&]*)
```

This rule reads that character data can be any character string excluding (^) the less-than symbol (<), the ampersand (&), and the]]> string.

4. [^abc],[^#xN#xN#xN]

Matches any character not defined.

The ISO/IEC 10646 defines a character as a specified unit, such as a tab, Latin A, etc.

See also the Unicode Standard.

Example:

Character data (Production Rule 14) is defined as:

```
CharData ::= [^<&]* - ([^<&]* ']]>' [^<&]*)
```

Character data is all text excluding markup that is the less-than symbol (<), the ampersand (&), and the]]> string.

5. "string"

Matches a literal string within double quotes.

For a match, the compared strings must be identical within ISO/IEC 10646 code definitions.

Example from Production Rule 11:

```
SystemLiteral ::= ('"' [^"]* '"') | ("'" [^']* "'")
```

Note: The first (expression) is this rule. For ease of reading, here is the example including spaces. SystemLiteral ::= (' " ' [^ "] ' " ') | (" ' " [^ '] " ' "). A string can be delimited by a set of double quotation marks.

6. 'string'

Matches a literal string within single quotes.

For a match, the compared strings must be identical within ISO/IEC 10646 code definitions.

Example from Production Rule 11:

```
SystemLiteral ::= ('"' [^"]* '"') | ("'" [^']* "'")
```

Note: The second (expression) is this rule. For ease of reading, here is the example including spaces. SystemLiteral ::= (' " ' [^ "] ' " ') | (" ' " [^ '] " ' "). A string can be delimited by a set of single quotation marks.

7. (expression)

A set of simple expressions treated as a unit within parentheses.

A (B) means A followed by the expression B. Production Rule 6 states:

```
Names ::= Name (S Name)*
```

This rule reads that Names has at least one Name followed by optional one or more occurrences of Name.

8. A?

   Matches A or nothing. Commonly used in production rules as S?. This means there can be zero or one occurrence of white space. Using the break (br) tag from HTML, one can have either <br/> or <br /> because this is an empty-element tag (Production Rule 44 for EmptyElemTag).

9. A B

   Matches A followed by B.

   Production Rule 1 states:

   ```
   document ::= prolog element Misc*
   ```

   This rule reads a document consisting of a prolog followed by an element and perhaps followed by miscellaneous markup.

10. A | B

    Matches A or B, but not both.

    Production Rule 3 reads:

    ```
    S ::= (#x20 | #x9 | #xD | #xA)+
    ```

    This rules that a white space (S) can be in hexadecimal a space (#x20) or (|) a tab (#x9) or (|) a carriage return (#xD) or (|) a line feed (#xA), and there must be an occurrence (+) for a white space to exist.

11. A - B

    Matches any string that matches A, but not B.

    Production Rule 17 for a processing instruction target reads:

    ```
    PITarget ::= Name - (('X' | 'x') ('M' | 'm') ('L' | 'l'))
    ```

    This rule reads that a name for a processing instruction name (PITarget) can be any name except one beginning with XML, xml, or any other combination of these six letters.

Note: See Production Rule 23 for a XMLDecl (XML Declaration).

12. A+

    There must be a match or matches of occurrence A.

    Production Rule 3 reads:

```
S ::= (#x20 | #x9 | #xD | #xA)+
```

This rules that a white space (S) can be in hexadecimal a space , a tab, a carriage return, or a line feed, and there must be an occurrence (+) for a white space to exist.

13. A*

Expression may occur or have occurrences.

Production Rule 1 reads:

```
document ::= prolog element Misc*
```

Misc* can occur or not occur and there still be a document.

14. /* ... */

This is a notation for commenting on a production rule. Production Rule 15 declares the syntax for a comment within XML markup. Comments can appear anywhere in a document except within markup.

```
Comment ::= '<!--' ((Char - '-') | ('-' (Char - '-')))* '-->'
```

Example:

```
<!-- This is an example comment. -->
```

15. [wfc: ...]

Well-formedness constraint

This identifies by name a constraint that can produce a fatal error. There are 10 of these constraints.

16. [vc: ...]

Validity constraint

This identifies by name a constraint that can produce an error that can be reported by a validating XML processor. There are 21 of these constraints.

Note: The SGML Standard uses X and Y instead of A and B as given above.

Ten of the key words of XML based on the Recommendation are:

■ Attribute

■ Constraint

■ Content

■ Declaration

- Element
- Entity
- Processing instruction
- Production rule
- Valid document
- Well-formed document

 Note: These words or concepts are discussed throughout the book. Also see Appendix A, "Terms and Definitions."

XML Benefits

XML is important for two types of applications: document or data exchange and database connectivity. XML provides a richer set of elements and publishing extensions than HTML. XML can handle application design for processing data that is for a specific use, but has a process that is an open, nonproprietary solution. The premise of this book is that a document should be considered a data object and thus can be processed in a CORBA networking environment as any object.

XML was designed to handle the foundational abilities of the object technology, similar to Java. Java's three key abilities are:

- Reusability
- Portability
- Interoperability

A key capability of XML is to handle interchange format transfer of data between different databases and different operating systems.

XML and SGML Comparison

XML is a child of SGML. The key to working with XML and SGML is ensuring that a DTD design works with both markup languages. This means that any SGML DTD should conform to XML production rules.[1]

---

1   While a comparison is done here, one must remember XML <u>is</u> SGML.

Note: An SGML DTD contains the pointers to the files with the DTD rules that govern the document's markup.

There are a number of differences between XML and SGML. Here are ten major differences:

■ XML requires both a start-tag and an end-tag, but SGML does not.

■ XML permits optional DTDs, but SGML does not.

■ XML is more flexible than SGML in expressing an element's rank in nests.

■ XML does not have declarations that are independent of the DTD and contain instructions for the parser.

■ XML does not have limitations on the quantity or capacity of document objects as SGML does.

■ XML comments require both <!-- and -->.

■ XML permits flexibility with default settings, but SGML uses the default of CURRENT.

■ XML is not as rich in features as SGML.

■ XML has speedier processing capabilities.

■ XML was designed for general use; SGML's complexity has resulted in use by documentation experts.

XML and HTML Comparison

While both XML and HTML are both markup language and are children of SGML, each has different generalizations and purposes. Because one knows HTML does not necessarily imply one knows XML.

XML uses most of the HTML tags, but a key requirement is the need to have both a start-tag and an end-tag. This means every <p> must have a </p>. There are three other required steps to ensure that an HTML document becomes a well-formed document (see Chapter 2 for a discussion of well-formedness processor constraints). The requirements are:

■ Tags must be nested correctly.

■ Attribute values must be within quotation marks (single or double).

■ Empty-elements must be correctly formatted.

HTML is a markup language that describes a document's structure, but is not designed for document format control. Frames were developed as a solution for this issue, but the two most common browsers, Microsoft's Internet Explorer and Netscape's Navigator, support frames differently.

Note: Many of the formatting controls (frames, tables, and new tags) were developed for HTML because of demands by Web designers. These designers never took the time to understand the basic concepts of HTML. This appears also to be happening to XML. However, this trend may not be blamed necessarily on designers.

XML was designed to do what HTML cannot:

■ Control document display.

■ Define complex links (multiple link declarations).

■ Describe different and specific document types.

■ Publish data in various forms of media.

■ Transport information in a various forms of media.

Perhaps the key difference between XML and HTML can be summed up in the word *extensible*. Extensible means that one can create one's own tags and attributes. One can also alter tags already defined in an existing document type definition (DTD). For example, Name could be declared a tag with two nested tags:

```
<!ELEMENT Name (LastName, FirstName) >
```

Note: There are dangers in this activity. These dangers are discussed in more detail in Chapter 10.

XML and Java Comparison

XML is an object-oriented markup language while Java is an object-oriented controlling programming language. Both were designed on the same three key principles:

■ Interoperability

■ Portability

■ Reusability

There are two methods to associate or link XML with Java. Both are under dynamic changes and one should check the Sun Microsystems (**www.sun.com**), Microsoft (**msdn.microsoft.com**), and World Wide Web Consortium (**www.w3.org/Style/XSL**) Web sites for the latest information. The methods are:

■ Use the Extensible Stylesheet Language (XSL) and JavaScript.

■ Use an XML parser with a Java compiler

Note: These two methods are discussed in more detail in Chapter 10.

XSL is in the proposal stage with the World Wide Web Consortium. XSL uses the underpinning concepts of Document Style Semantics and Specification Language (DSSSL), an ISO standard. The basic goals of XSL are:

■ To be used over the Internet

■ To be readable by a human

■ To be created easily

XSL uses a variant of JavaScript. The variant includes features for applying style to Web documents. XSL focuses on document style applications. XSL with XML has the ability to fetch data from a document and present the data with a desired style.

The second method of using an XML parser and a Java compiler is first based on the premise that applications with XML require an XML parser. The second premise is that programmers use either a command-line interface or an application programming interface (API) to include parsing. Third, XML builds information interchange languages. And finally, the use of the notion of an Object Model Interface is a keystone factor of this method.

Note: The goal of this technology is the integration of the Document Object Model and the API. The Web site for the latest is: **www.w3.org/DOM/**.

Chapter 2

XML Design Policy

> ### Included in This Chapter:
>
> - ❏ Some Related Internet Sites
> - ❏ Production Rules Overview
> - ❏ Well-Formed Documents
> - ❏ Valid Documents
> - ❏ Document Structure
> - ❏ Logical Structure
> - ❏ Physical Structure
> - ❏ XML Processor Guidelines

For purposes of discussion, a policy can consist of recommendations (may do this), specifications or rules (shall do this), structure (parameters are this and not that), and guidelines (steps to do this). The ultimate goal of an XML design policy is for a developed XML document to have a conforming XML processor return no error messages. Structure, not appearance, is the underpinning concept for XML design. There are other "X languages" that establish relationships, pointers, and presentation.

To achieve an error-free goal, one needs to be knowledgeable of the XML production rules, the processor constraints and guidelines, and the logical and physical structures of XML documents. The underpinnings of these items are ten design goals for XML. The key goals for XML are to be usable over the Internet, to support a wide variety of applications, to be compatible with

SGML, and to have a minimal set of optional features. Other goals are that XML design can be written easily, be prepared quickly, and be formal (organized) and concise. XML documents should be human-legible and should be easy to create. The tenth goal reflects the growth of storage capacity: "Terseness in XML markup is of minimal importance."[1]

Note: Based on the tenth goal, an XML markup commandment is "Thy markup shall be commented."

There are 89 production rules. These rules have over 500 permutations. This book's focus is on some of the key permutations to show how XML can be applicable to CORBA.

Note: This chapter relies heavily on the production rules to give a foundational basis for further discussions on how to implement them. The place and order of a production rule is important in an implementing context.

There are two types of processor constraints: well-formedness and validity. They are the consequences for failure to adhere to the production rules. These constraints are the basis for the design of the functions of a conforming XML processor. A conforming processor must follow or adhere to the well-formedness constraints in the Extensible Markup Language (XML) 1.0 W3 Recommendation (10 February 1998).

A well-formedness constraint is a rule that when not adhered to produces a fatal error and a conforming XML processor <u>must</u> report to the application. The process terminates and gives a message. The process cannot continue to pass character data and information about the document's logical structure to the application in the normal way.

A validity constraint is a rule that when not adhered to produces an error where the results are unpredictable. The conforming processor may detect and report an error and may recover from it. Validating XML processors <u>must</u> report the errors at user option.

---

[1] A goal of the W3C XML Activity was to write a concise document. The XML Recommendation is a set of 89 conclusions, or production rules, without alternatives and with minimal comments. Experts in the field of publishing technology, such as SGML, established these rules after lengthy discussions. One also needs a high level of knowledge of computer science because of the technical jargon used, such as production, declaration, and token.

Note: This chapter relies heavily on the precise language of the XML Recommendation 1.0 (10 February 1998). Other chapters explain these rules in language that is appropriate to this book's objectives.

This chapter closes with guidelines on how a processor should handle the production rules. These rules state the implications of all of the production rules. These guidelines can be considered a supplement of the well-formedness and validity constraints.

Some Related Internet Sites

These sites are directly related to the Recommendation. Other sites are listed in Appendix E.

www.w3.org/XML (for XML activity)

www.w3.org/TR (other recommendations)

www.w3.org/XML/xml-19980210-errata (for errors)

ftp://nic.ddn.mil/rfc/rfcNNNN.txt (NNNN is RFC number; see 1766 for language ID tags)

charts.unicode.org/ (canonical code values)

Production Rules Overview

As stated previously, there are 89 production rules, and these rules have over 500 permutations. These rules can be classified in four general areas: document definition (Rules 1-38), logical document structure (Rules 39-65), physical document structure (Rules 66-83), and character definition (Rules 84-89). The rules comply with the Extended Backus-Naur Form (EBNF) notation. The rule form is:

```
symbol ::= expression
```

Also included with some rules are processor constraints, well-formedness and validity. These constraints are at times further clarified "for compatibility" and "for interoperability." These clarifications relate to XML's relationship to SGML.

These production rules were designed and developed to implement the ten XML goals given in the second paragraph of this chapter. It may be a semantic issue but this book refers to XML production rules rather than XML as syntax. XML permits you to create your own markup tags. You are not limited to using or distorting tags with specified syntax as with SGML or more particularly HTML.

Note: All the production rules are listed in Appendix C.

Well-Formed Documents

Five steps in achieving well-formedness for parsed entities:

1. All internal parameter entities are well-formed by definition.
2. The well-formed document entity matches the production document (Rule 1).
3. A well-formed internal general parsed entity's replacement text matches the production content (Rule 43).
4. A well-formed external general parsed entity matches the production extParsedEnt (Rule 78).

    Rule 78:

    ```
    extParsedEnt ::= TextDecl? Content
    ```

5. A well-formed external parameter entity matches the production extPE (Rule 79).

    Rule 79:

    ```
    extPE ::= TextDecl? ExtSubsetDecl
    ```

Note: Rules 78 and 79 use Rules 31 (ExtSubsetDecl), 43 (Content), and 77 (TextDecl).

A consequence of well-formedness in entities is the logical and physical structures in an XML document are properly nested. This means that no start-tag, end-tag, empty-element tag, element, comment, processing instruction, character reference, or entity reference can begin in one entity and end in another.

Note: See Rules 15, 16, 39, 40, 42, 44, 66, and 68 for details.

There are ten well-formedness constraints in the Recommendation. If a well-formedness constraint is <u>not</u> adhered to, there is a fatal error and a conforming processor must give notification and terminate its processing.

Note: These constraints are listed in Appendix D and are more detailed with their associated production rules.

Valid Documents

A valid XML document complies with the stated validity constraints. There are 21 validity constraints in the Recommendation. If a validity constraint is <u>not</u> adhered to, the result is unpredictable. A validating processor must report validity constraint failures.

Note: These constraints are listed in Appendix D and are more detailed with their associated production rules.

Document Structure

An XML document basically consists of:

■ A root document entity

Rule 1:

```
document ::= prolog element Misc*
```

■ Declarations (in logical and physical structures)
■ Comments

Rule 15:

```
Comment ::= '<!- -' ((Char - '-') | ('-' (Char - '-')))* '- ->'
```

Example of a comment:

```
<!- - This is a comment example. - ->
```

■ Character references
■ Processing instructions

Rule 16:

```
PI ::= '<?' PI Target (S (Char* - (Char*  '?>' Char*)))? '?>'
```

- Elements (logical structure, Rules 39-65)
- Entities (physical structure, Rules 66-83)

Logical Structure

The logical structure of an XML document is indicated by explicit markup known as elements bounded by:

- Start-tags
- End-tags
- Empty-element tags

Rules for Element Type Declarations

An element is the core component of the logical structure. The key characteristics of an element are:

- Has a type, identified by name (generic identifier (GI)).
- May have a set of attribute specifications, each with a unique name and value.

An element is defined by Rule 39:

```
element ::= EmptyElemTag | STag content ETag
                [ WFC: Element Type Match ]
                [ VC: Element Valid ]
```

When an element has content, text, a start-tag, and an end-tag must delimit the content. When an element is empty, it must be represented either by a start-tag immediately followed by an end-tag or by an empty-element tag.

Well-Formedness Constraint: Element Type Match means the name in an element's end-tag must match the element type in the start-tag.

Validity Constraint: Element Valid means there must be a declaration matching elementdecl (Rule 45) where the name (Rule 5) matches the element type and one of the following holds:

- The declaration matches EMPTY and the element has no content.
- The declaration matches children (Rule 47) and the child element sequence belongs to the content model language, with optional white space (Rule 3) between each child element.
- The declaration matches MIXED (Rule 51) and the content consists of character data (Rule 14) and child elements whose types match names in the content model.
- The declaration matches ANY, and the types of any child elements have been declared.

Note: Rule 39 uses production Rules 40, 41, 43, and 44.

The start-tag appearing at the beginning of a non-empty element has two production rules:

Rule 40:

```
STag ::= '<' Name (S Attribute)* S? '>'
            [ WFC: Unique Att Spec ]
```

Rule 41:

```
Attribute ::= Name Eq AttValue
            [ VC: Attribute Value Type ]
            [ WFC: No External Entity Reference ]
            [ WFC: No < in Attribute Values ]
```

Notes: (Rules 40 and 41):

- Element's type is the Name between the start-tag and end-tag.
- An attribute specification is a Name-AttValue pair.
- Well-Formedness Constraint: Unique Att Spec means an attribute name can appear <u>once</u> in the same start-tag or empty-element tag.
- Validity Constraint: Attribute Value Type means the attribute <u>must</u> have been declared. The value <u>must</u> be of the type declared for it.
- Well-Formedness Constraint: No External Entity Reference means an attribute value cannot contain entity references to external entities.

■ An attribute value is the content or text between the 'or' delimiters.

■ Well-Formedness Constraint: No < in Attribute Values means the replacement text of a referenced entity in an attribute value (other than "<") <u>must</u> not contain a <.

The end-tag, which echoes the start-tag, appearing at the end of a non-empty element has this production rule:

Rule 42:

```
ETag ::= '</' Name S? '>'
```

Example of a start-tag and end-tag:

```
<termdef id="dt-CORBAservices" term="Opposite of CORBAfacilities.">
</termdef>
```

The content of elements is the text between the start-tag and the end-tag.

Rule 43:

```
content ::= (element | CharData | Reference | CDSect | PI | Comment)*
```

Note: Rules 14, 15, 16, 18, 39, and 67 and are used in this rule definition.

Rule for Empty Elements

The tag for an empty element is a special form used for an element without content. It serves the same function as a start-tag followed by an end-tag. It <u>must</u> be used when an element is declared EMPTY.

Rule 44:

```
EmptyElemTag ::= '<' Name (S Attribute)* S? '/>'
                      [ WFC: Unique Att Spec ]
```

Well-Formedness Constraint: Unique Att Spec means a name can appear <u>once</u> in the same start-tag or empty-element tag.

Rules for Element Types

The element structure for an XML document for validation purposes can be defined or constrained (boundaries established) using element type (Rules 45 and 46) and attribute-list declarations (Rules 52 and 53).

An element type declaration can also establish the constraints of an element's children (Rule 47).

Note: At the user's option, an XML processor can issue a warning when a declaration mentions an element type that has no declaration.

An element type declaration takes the form:

Rule 45:

```
elementdecl ::= '<!ELEMENT' S Name S contentspec S? '>'
                       [ VC: Unique Element Type Declaration ]
```

Validity Constraint: Unique Element Type Declaration means no element may be declared more than once.

Rule 46:

```
contentspec ::= '<!EMPTY' | 'ANY' | Mixed | children
```

Note: The Name gives the element type being declared.

Examples of Element Type Declarations:

```
<!ELEMENT br EMPTY>
```

```
<!ELEMENT container ANY>
```

```
<!ELEMENT p (#PCDATA|emph)* >
```

```
<!ELEMENT %name.para; %content.para; >
```

Rules for Element Contents

Element content is when an element type can contain only child elements, no character data, optionally separated by white space (Rule 3).

The option requires a content model, a grammar that governs the allowed child element types and the order of their appearance. The grammar is based on content particles (cps) (Rule 48).

Four element-content models are:

Rule 47:

```
children ::= (choice | seq) ('?' | '*' | '+')?
```

Rule 48:

```
cp ::= (Name | choice | seq) ('?' | '*' | '+')?
```

Rule 49:

```
choice ::= '(' S? cp ( S? '|' S? cp )* S? ')'
           [ VC: Proper Group/PE Nesting ]
```

Rule 50:

```
seq ::= '(' S? cp ( S? ',' S? cp )* S? ')'
        [ VC: Proper Group/PE Nesting ]
```

Validity Constraint: Proper Group/PE Nesting means parameter-entity replacement text must be properly nested within parentheses.

For interoperability, if a parameter-entity reference appears in a choice, seq, or Mixed construct, its replacement text should <u>not</u> be empty. A connector (| or ,) should <u>not</u> be the first nor last non-blank character of the replacement text.

Examples of Element content models:

```
<!ELEMENT div1 (head, (p | list | note)*, div2*)>
<!ELEMENT spec (front, body, back?)>
<!ELEMENT dictionary-body (%div.mix; | %dict.mix;)*>
```

Note: The content of an element matches a content model if it is possible to trace out a path through the content model, obeying the sequence, choice, and repetition operators and matching each element in the content against an element type in the content model.

For compatibility, it is an error if an element in the document matches more than one occurrence of an element type in the content model.

Rule for Mixed Content

Mixed content is when an element type <u>may</u> contain character data, optionally interspersed with child elements. The types of child elements may be constrained, but not their order or their number of occurrences. A mixed-content declaration requires that the name(s) give the types of elements that may appear as children.

Rule 51:

```
Mixed ::= '(' S? '#PCDATA' (S? '|' S? Name)* S? ')*' | '(' S?
            '#PCDATA' S? ')'
         [ VC: Proper Group/PE Nesting ]
         [ VC: No Duplicate Types ]
```

Validity Constraint: Proper Group/PE Nesting means parameter-entity replacement text must be properly nested within parentheses.

For interoperability, if a parameter-entity reference appears in a choice, seq, or Mixed construct, its replacement text should not be empty. A connector (| or ,) should not be the first nor last non-blank character of the replacement text.

Validity Constraint: No Duplicate Types means the same name must not appear more than once in a single mixed-content declaration.

Examples of mixed-content declarations:

```
<!ELEMENT p (#PCDATA|a|ul|b|i|em)*>
<!ELEMENT p (#PCDATA | %font; | %phrase; | %special; | %form;)* >
<!ELEMENT b (#PCDATA)>
```

Rules for Element Attributes

An attribute (Rule 41) associates a name-value pair with an element (Rule 39). An attribute specification appears only within a start-tag or an element tag.

An attribute-list declaration specifies the name, data type, and default value (if any) of each attribute associated with a given element. An attribute-list declaration may:

■ Define the set of attributes pertaining to a given element type.

■ Establish type constraints for these attributes.

■ Provide default values for attributes.

In an attribute-list declaration, the Name in the AttlistDecl Rule (52) is the type of element. Name in the AttDef Rule (53) is the name of the attribute.

Rule 52:

```
AttlistDecl ::= '<!ATTLIST' S Name AttDef* S? '>'
```

Rule 53:

```
AttDef ::= S Name S AttType S DefaultDecl
```

Note: AttType is Rule 54. DefaultDecl is Rule 60.

For interoperability, a DTD can have:

■ One attribute-list declaration for a given element type.
■ One attribute definition for a given attribute name.
■ One or more attribute definitions in an attribute-list declaration.

Rules for Attribute Types

There are three kinds of attribute types:

■ A string type (Rule 55)
■ A tokenized type (Rule 56)
■ An enumerated type (Rules 57-59)

Rule 54:

```
AttType ::= StringType | TokenizedType | Enumerated Type
```

The string type may take any literal string as a value.

Rule 55:

```
StringType ::= 'CDATA'
```

The tokenized type has a variety of lexical and semantic constraints.

Rule 56:

```
TokenizedType ::= 'ID'[ VC: ID ]
                  [ VC: One ID per Element Type ]
                  [ VC: ID Attribute Default ]
                  | 'IDREF'[ VC: IDREF ]
                  | 'IDREFS'[ VC: IDREF ]
                  | 'ENTITY'[ VC: Entity Name ]
                  | 'ENTITIES'[ VC: Entity Name ]
                  | 'NMTOKEN'[ VC: Name Token ]
                  | 'NMTOKENS'[ VC: Name Token ]
```

Notes:

- Validity Constraint: ID means values of the type ID <u>must</u> match the Name production (Rule 5). ID values <u>must</u> uniquely identify the elements that bear them.

- Validity Constraint: One ID per Element Type means an element type <u>must</u> have only one ID specified attribute.

- Validity Constraint: ID Attribute Default means an ID attribute <u>must</u> have a declared default of #IMPLIED or #REQUIRED.

- Validity Constraint: IDREF means values of types IDREF and IDREFS MUST match Name and Names production respectively (Rules 5 and 6). IDREF values <u>must</u> match the value of some ID attribute.

- Validity Constraint: Entity Name means values of types ENTITY and ENTITIES <u>must</u> match Name and Names production (Rules 5 and 6).

  Each Name <u>must</u> match the name of an unparsed entity (Rule 66) declared in the DTD.

- Validity Constraint: Name Token means values of types NMTOKEN and NMTOKENS <u>must</u> match Nmtoken and Nmtokens production (Rules 7 and 8).

Rules for Enumerated Types

There are two kinds of enumerated types. They have a variety of attributes as determined by the declaration.

Rule 57:

```
EnumeratedType ::= NotationType | Enumeration
```

Rule 58:

```
NotationType ::= 'NOTATION' S '(' S? Name (S? | S? Name)* S? ')'
                 [ VC: Notation Attribute ]
```

Rule 59:

```
Enumeration ::= '(' S? Nmtoken (S? '|' S? Nmtoken)*
                [ VC: Enumeration ]
```

Notes:

- A NOTATION attribute identifies a notation, declared in the DTD with associated system and/or public identifiers, to be used in interpreting the element to which the attribute is attached.
- A notation identifies by name the format of an unparsed entity.
- For interoperability, the same Nmtoken <u>must</u> occur only once in the enumerated types of an element type.
- Validity Constraint: Notation Attribute means Values of this type <u>must</u> match one of the notation names included in the declaration; all notation names in the declaration <u>must</u> be declared.
- Validity Constraint: Enumeration means values of this type <u>must</u> match one of the Nmtoken tokens in the declaration.

Rule for Attribute Defaults

Rule 53 (AttDef) contains DefaultDecl; it is for declaring an attribute default. If an attribute declaration does not provide whether the attribute's presence is required, DefaultDecl is used.

Rule 60:

```
DefaultDecl ::= '#REQUIRED' | '#IMPLIED' | (('FIXED' S )? AttValue)
                [ VC: Required Attribute ]
                [ VC: Attribute Default Legal ]
                [ WFC: No < in Attribute Values]
                [ VC: Fixed Attribute Default ]
```

Notes:

- Validity Constraint: Required Attribute means that when the default is #REQUIRED, the attribute <u>must</u> be specified for <u>all</u> elements of the type in the attribute-list declaration (Rule 52).
- Validity Constraint: Attribute Default Legal means the declared default value <u>must</u> meet the lexical constraints of the declared attribute type (Rule 54).
- Well-Formedness Constraint: No < in Attribute Values means the replacement text of a referenced entity in an attribute value (other than "<") <u>must</u> not contain a <.

■ Validity Constraint: Fixed Attribute Default means when the default is #FIXED, the instances of that attribute <u>must</u> match the default value.

Examples of attribute-list declarations:

```
<!ATTLIST termdef
     id ID #REQUIRED
     name CDATA #IMPLIED>
<!ATTLIST list
     type (bullets|ordered|glossary) "ordered">
<!ATTLIST form
     method CDATA #FIXED "POST">
  -
```

Notes:

■ #REQUIRED means that the attribute <u>must</u> be provided.

■ #IMPLIED mean no default value is provided.

■ #FIXED means that the attribute <u>must</u> have a default value.

The processor must normalize an attribute value before it is checked for validity or passed to an application. Normalization is as follows:

■ A character reference is processed by appending it to the attribute value.

■ An entity reference is processed by recursively processing the replacement text of the entity.

■ White space (Rule 3) is processed by appending a single #x20.

■ Other characters are processed by appending them to the normalized value.

Notes:

■ If the declared value is <u>not</u> CDATA, then the XML processor <u>must</u> further process the normalized attribute value by discarding any leading and trailing space (#x20) characters, and by replacing sequences of space (#x20) characters by a single space (#x20) character.

■ A non-validating parser should treat all attributes for which no declaration has been read as if declared CDATA.

Rules for Conditional Sections

Conditional sections (Rules 61-65) are portions of the DTD external subset that are included in or excluded from the DTD's logical structure based on the keyword that governs them.

Rule 61:

```
conditionalSect ::= includeSect | ignoreSect
```

Rule 62:

```
includeSect ::= '<![' S? 'INCLUDE' S? '[' extSubsetDecl ']]>'
```

Rule 63:

```
ignoreSect ::= '<![' S? 'IGNORE' S? '[' ignoreSectContents ']]>'
```

Rule 64:

```
ignoreSectContents ::= Ignore ('<![' ignoreSectContents ']]>' Ignore)*
```

Rule 65:

```
Ignore ::= Char* - (Char* ('<![' | ']]>') Char*)
```

Example of conditional sections:

```
<!ENTITY %draft 'INCLUDE'>
<!ENTITY %final 'IGNORE'>

<![%draft;[
<!ELEMENT book (comments*, title, body, supplements?)>
]]>
<![%final;[
<!ELEMENT book (title, body, supplements?)>
]]>
-
```

Notes:

■ A conditional section may contain one or more complete declarations, comments, processing instructions, or nested conditional sections, intermingled with white space.

■ INCLUDE means the contents of the conditional section are part of the DTD.

Physical Structure

The physical structure of an XML document consists of entities. Entities are storage units that have content. All are identified by name except the document entity and the external DTD subset. There is only one document entity.

Entities are either parsed or unparsed. A parsed entity's contents are referred to as its replacement text. This text is an integral part of the document. A parsed entity is invoked by name using entity references.

An unparsed entity's contents may or may not be text. The text may not be XML. An unparsed entity does have an associated notation (Rule 82) identified by name. An unparsed entity is invoked by name given in the value of ENTITY or ENTITIES attributes.

An entity can be general or a parameter. A general entity is for use within the document content. A parameter entity is for use within the DTD. Because they occupy different namespaces, a general entity and a parameter entity with the same name are distinctive.

Rule for Character References

A character reference refers to a specific character in the ISO/IEC 10646 character set. That is one not directly accessible from available input devices.

Rule 66:

```
CharRef ::= '&#' [0-9]+ ';' | '&#x' [0-9a-fA-F]+ ';'
              [ WFC: Legal Character ]
```

Well-Formedness Constraint: Legal Character means characters referred to using character references <u>must</u> match the production of Char (Rule 2).

If the character reference begins with "&#x", the digits and letters up to the terminating semicolon (;) provide a hexadecimal representation of the character code point in ISO/IEC 10646. If it begins with "&#", the digits up to the terminating semicolon (;) provide a decimal representation.

Rules for Entity References

An entity reference refers to the content of a named entity. Parsed general entity references use as delimiters the ampersand (&) and semicolon (;). Parameter-entity references use as delimiters the percent sign (%) and semicolon (;). Entity reference is governed by Rules 67-69.

Rule 67:

```
Reference ::= EntityRef | CharRef
```

Rule 68:

```
EntityRef ::= '&' Name ';'
              [WFC: Entity Declared ]
              [VC: Entity Declared ]
              [ WFC: Parsed Entity ]
              [ WFC: No Recursion ]
```

Rule 69:

```
PEReference ::= '%' Name ';'
                [ VC: Entity Declared ]
                [ WFC: No Recursion]
                [ WFC: In DTD ]
```

Well-Formedness Constraint: In a document without a DTD, a document with only an internal DTD subset which contains no parameter entity references, or a document with "standalone='yes'", Entity Declared means the Name given in the entity reference <u>must</u> match that in an entity declaration. However, there is an exception. Well-formed documents need not declare amp, lt, gt, apos, or quot.

Validity Constraint: In a document with an external subset or external parameter entities with "standalone='no'", Entity Declared means the Name given in the entity references <u>must</u> match that in an entity declaration.

For interoperability, valid documents should declare the entities amp, lt, gt, apos, or quot in the specified form.

Well-Formedness Constraint: Parsed Entity means an entity reference <u>must</u> not contain the name of an unparsed entity. However, unparsed entities may be referred to only in attribute values (Rule 10) declared to be of type ENTITY or ENTITIES.

Well-Formedness Constraint: No Recursion means a parsed entity <u>must</u> not contain a recursive reference to itself, either directly or indirectly.

Well-Formedness Constraint: In DTD means Parameter-entity references may only appear in the DTD.

Example of character and entity references:

```
Type <key>less-than</key> (&#x3C;) to save options.
This document was prepared on &docdate; and is
classified &security-level;.
```

Example of parameter-entity reference:

```
<! declare the parameter entity "ISOLat2"... >
<!ENTITY %ISOLat2
        SYSTEM "hhtp://www.xml.com/iso/isolat2-xml.entities">
<! ... now reference it >
%ISOLat2
```

Rules for Internal Entities

An entity declaration is governed by five production rules (Rules 70-74). The Name in the rules identifies the entity in an entity reference (Rule 68) or, in the case of an unparsed entity, in the value of an ENTITY or ENTITIES attribute.

Note: The first declaration occurrence of an entity is binding.

Rule 70:

```
EntityDecl ::= GEDecl | PEDecl
```

Rule 71:

```
GEDecl ::= '<!ENTITY' S Name S EntityDef S? '>'
```

Rule 72:

```
PEDecl ::= '<!ENTITY' S '%' S Name S PEDef S? '>'
```

Rule 73:

```
EntityDef ::= EntityValue | (ExternalID NDataDecl?)
```

Rule 74:

```
PEDef ::= EntityValue | ExternalID
```

An internal entity is when the entity definition is an EntityValue (Rule 9). There is no separate physical storage object, and the content of the entity is given in declaration. An internal entity is a parsed entity.

Example of an internal entity declaration:

```
<!ENTITY Pub-Status "This is a pre-release of the specification">
```

Rules for External Entity Declarations

An external entity is an entity that is not a part of the internal markup declarations. There is no entity definition that is an EntityValue (Rule 9). There are two production rules (Rules 75-76). If the NDATADecl (Rule 76) is present, a general unparsed entity exists; otherwise, it is a parsed entity.

Rule 75:

```
ExternalID ::= 'SYSTEM' S SystemLiteral | 'PUBLIC' S PubidLiteral
                    S SystemLiteral
```

Rule 76:

```
NDataDecl ::= S 'NDATA' S Name
                [ VC: Notation Declared ]
```

Notes:

■ Validity Constraint: Notation Declared means the Name <u>must</u> match the declared name of notation (Rule 82).

■ The SystemLiteral is called the entity's system identifier.

■ The PubidLiteral is an external identifier, public.

Examples of external entity declarations:

```
<!ENTITY galley
      SYSTEM "http://www.myplace.com/template/Galley.xml">
<!ENTITY galley
      PUBLIC "-//Myplace//TEXT Standard galley template//EN"
      "http://www.myplace.com/template/Galley.xml">
<!ENTITY galley
      SYSTEM "../grafix/Galley.gif"
      NDATA gif>
```

Rule for Text Declarations

A parsed entity is invoked by name using an entity reference. It is an integral part of the document. Its contents are referred to as replacement text.

A text declaration can only appear at the beginning of an external parsed entity. A text declaration <u>must</u> be provided literally, not by reference to a parsed entity.

Rule 77:

```
TextDecl ::= '<?xml' VersionInfo? EncodingDecl S? '?>'
```

Note: This rule uses Rules 3, 24, and 80.

Rules for Notation Declarations

Notations identify by name the format of unparsed entities, the format of elements that bear a notation attribute, or the application to which a processing instruction is addressed.

Notation declarations provide a name for the notation for use in entity and attribute-list declarations and in attribute specifications and an external identifier for the notation which may allow an XML processor or its client application to locate a helper application capable of processing data in the given notation.

Rule 82:

```
NotationDecl ::='<NOTATION' S Name S (ExternalID | PublicID) S? '>'
```

Rule 83:

```
PublicID ::= 'PUBLIC' S PubidLiteral
```

XML processors <u>must</u> provide applications with the name and external identifier(s) of any notation declared and referred to in an attribute value, an attribute definition, or an entity declaration.

XML Processor Guidelines

Processor guidelines are precise statements on how a conforming processor shall implement the productions. The guidelines supplement the well-formedness and validity constraints. Why do you need to be aware of these guidelines? Your ultimate goal as a designer is to have error-free XML markup.

Character Encoding Guidelines

The requirements for processors to do character encoding in entities are:

1. Each external parsed entity may use different encoding.
2. All XML processors <u>must</u> be able to read entities in either UTF-8 or UTF-16.
3. The XML processor <u>must</u> use the Byte Order Mark described by ISO/IEC 10646 to differentiate between UTF-16 (beginning code) and UTF-8.
4. Parsed entities using encoding other than UTF-8 and UTF-16 <u>must</u> begin with a text declaration containing an encoding declaration.
5. In the document entity, the encoding declaration is part of the XML declaration (Rule 23).
6. The EncName (Rule 81) is the name of the encoding used.

The encoding declaration rules are:

Rule 80:

```
EncodingDecl ::= S 'encoding' Eq ('"' EncName '"'  | "'" EncName "'" )
```

Rule 81:

```
EncName ::= [A-Za-z] ([A-Za-z0-9._] | '-')*
```

Note: Encoding name contains only Latin characters.

Examples of encoding declarations:

```
<?xml encoding='UTF-8'?>
<?xml encoding='ISO-10646-UCS-2'?>
<?xml encoding='ISO-8859-1'?>
<?xml encoding="EUC-JP"?>
```

Unparsed Entities Treatment Guidelines

Guidelines for an XML processor's treatment of unparsed entities are:

1. Reference in Content is anywhere after the start-tag and before the end-tag of an element. It corresponds to the non-terminal content.

2. Reference in Attribute Value is within either the value of an attribute in a start-tag or a default value in an attribute declaration. It corresponds to the non-terminal AttValue.

3. Attribute Value is a Name, not a reference. It appears either as the value of an attribute that has been declared as type ENTITY or as one of the space-separated tokens in the value of an attribute which has been declared as type ENTITIES.

4. Reference in Entity Value is within a parameter or internal entity's literal entity value in the entity's declaration. It corresponds to the non-terminal EntityValue.

5. Reference in DTD is within either the internal or external subsets of the DTD, but outside of an EntityValue or AttValue.

Not Recognized Guidelines

The Not Recognized guidelines are:

1. Outside of the DTD the percent (%) character has no special significance; thus, what would be parameter-entity references in the DTD are not recognized as markup in content.

2. The names of unparsed entities are not recognized except when they appear in the value of an appropriately declared attribute.

Included Guidelines

The Included guidelines are:

1. An entity is included when its replacement text is retrieved and processed, in place of the reference itself, as though it were part of the document at the location the reference was recognized.

2. The replacement text may contain both character data and (except for parameter entities) markup.

3. A character reference is included when the indicated character is processed in place of the reference itself.

Included if Validating Guidelines

The Included if Validating guidelines are:

1. For an XML processor to validate a document it <u>must</u> include the document's replacement text.

2. If a non-validating parser does not include the replacement text, it <u>must</u> inform the application that it recognized, but did not read, the entity.

Forbidden Guidelines

The Forbidden guidelines constitute <u>fatal</u> errors:

1. The appearance of a reference to an unparsed entity.

2. The appearance of any character or general-entity reference in the DTD except within an EntityValue or AttValue.

3. A reference to an external entity in an attribute value.

Included in Literal Guidelines

The Included in Literal guidelines are:

1. When an entity reference appears in an attribute value or a parameter-entity reference appears in a literal entity value, its replacement text is processed in place of the reference as though it were part of the document at the location the reference was recognized. There is an exception. A single- or double-quote character in the replacement text is treated as a normal data character and does not terminate the literal.

2. Well-formed:

```
<!ENTITY % YN '"Yes"' >
<!ENTITY WhatSheSaid "She said &YN;" >
```

3. Not well-formed:

```
<!ENTITY EndAttr "27'" >
<element attribute='a-&EndAttr;>
```

Notify Guideline

The Notify guideline is:

When the name of an unparsed entity appears as a token in the value of an attribute of declared type ENTITY or ENTITIES, a validating processor <u>must</u> inform the application of the system and public identifiers for both the entity and its associated notation.

Bypassed Guideline

The Bypassed guideline is:

When a general entity reference appears in the EntityValue in an entity declaration, it is bypassed and left as is.

Included as PE Guidelines

The Included as PE (parameter-entity) guidelines are:

1. Parameter entities need only be included if validating.
2. When a parameter-entity reference is recognized in the DTD and included, its replacement text is enlarged by the attachment of one leading and one following space (#x20) character. The intent is to constrain the replacement text of parameter entities to contain an integral number of grammatical tokens in the DTD.

Internal Entity Treatment Guideline

The Internal Entity Treatment guideline is:

The treatment of internal entities requires that an entity's value be considered in its two forms: literal entity value or replacement text. The literal entity value is the quoted string present in the entity declaration (non-terminal EntityValue).

The replacement text is the content of the entity after replacement of character references and parameter-entity references.

The internal entity value as given in EntityValue may contain these references:

■ Character
■ Parameter-entity
■ General-entity

The replacement text that is included <u>must</u> contain:

■ The replacement text of any parameter entities referred to.
■ The character referred to in place of any character references in the literal entity value.

The general-entity references <u>must</u> be left, unexpanded.

Predefined Entities Guidelines

The Predefined Entities guidelines are:

Entity and references can be used to escape the left angle bracket (<), ampersand (&), and other delimiters. These general entities have been specified for this purpose: amp, lt, gt, apos, and quot.

Numeric references are handled by "<" and "&". They are used to escape the left angle bracket (<) and ampersand (&) when they occur in character data.

Example declarations:

```
<!ENTITY lt "&#38;#60;">
<!ENTITY gt "&#62;">
<!ENTITY amp "&#38;&#38;">
<!ENTITY apos "&#39;">
<!ENTITY quot "&#34;">
```

Miscellaneous Guidelines

The document entity serves as the root of the entity and a starting point for an XML processor.

Conformance is concerned with whether a processor is validating or non-validating.

A processor <u>must</u> report any well-formedness constraint violations whether document entity or parsed entity.

Validating Process Guidelines

A validating processor must:

- Report violations of the declarations in the DTD (fatal errors).
- Report any validity constraint errors.
- Read and process the DTD and external referenced parsed entities.

A non-validating processor must:

- Report violations of the declarations in the DTD (fatal errors).
- Read and process the internal DTD subset and only parameters up to the first reference that cannot be read.

Users can be impacted by processor type, in particular the non-validating type.

- Certain well-formedness errors, specifically those that require reading external entities, may not be detected.
- Attribute values may not be normalized when information is passed from processor to an application.

Chapter 3

Developing an XML Document Type Definition (DTD)

Included in This Chapter:

❏ DTD FAQ

❏ What is a DTD?

❏ Document Logical Structure

❏ Document Physical Structure

❏ Markup Declarations Overview

❏ Developing a Model DTD

❏ Developing a Document Type Declaration

❏ Role of the Processor

This chapter looks at the fundamental process for developing a document type definition (DTD). The ideas given are extended in the chapters on developing DTDs for CORBA.

This chapter concludes with a discussion on the key tool for developing a DTD and XML documents, the parser (processor). In actuality there are three key tools: parsers, editors (your choice of a text editor), and browsers. Check the appropriate Web sites for the latest information on XML implementation by browser vendors since this is, to say the least, a dynamic area. It is also recommended to go beyond the parser discussion and do a search on "XML parser."

The following section has ten frequently asked questions about a DTD. The answers to these questions are expanded upon in other sections of this chapter.

DTD FAQ

1.   What is a document type definition?

An XML user can define the role of each element of text in a formal model, known as a document type definition (DTD). This action enables the user to declare where each component of document occurs in a valid place within the interchanged data stream.

An XML DTD enables a computer, that is, a parser, to check, for example, the logical structure of a document. A rule of a logical document structure is that a second-level heading is not entered prior to its associated first-level heading.

Note: Document structure logic is based on an evolutionary process that established the elements with their attributes and their order in a given document type. For example, the logical structure of a novel is different from a textbook. They may or may not have similar physical attributes such as font type and size.

XML does not require the presence of a DTD. When a DTD is not used, an XML system assigns a default definition for undeclared components of the markup.

Note: A default definition may enable one to use HTML tags when both the start-tags and end-tags are present.

2.   What are some types of document types (text structures) that can be defined by XML?

XML can describe any logical text structure: book, database, dictionary, encyclopedia, form, letter, memo, or report. It extends the notion of page. A spreadsheet can be a document type. Later in this chapter a general model DTD for an e-mail document type is developed.

3. What are three key logical components of an XML document?

   The three key logical components of an XML document are entity, element, and attribute. Each entity can contain one or more logical elements. Each of these elements can have certain attributes (properties) that describe the way in which it is to be processed.

4. What is the importance of the concept of document to XML?

   XML is based on the metaphor (an implicit designation) of a document composed of a series of entities (containers). In programming parlance the equivalent word would be object. Class is also an equivalent in some cases.

5. What is the important difference between XML and SGML?

   Simplistically, XML is an optimized markup language (subset) of SGML for the Web. XML is data-centric rather than publishing-centric.

6. What is an important difference between XML markup and HTML markup?

   An XML document must clearly mark where the start and end of each of the component parts occurs. The core rule in XML is start-tag, content, and end-tag; or an empty-element tag.

7. How does XML differ from other markup languages?

   XML differs from other markup languages in that it not only indicates where a change of appearance occurs or where a new element starts, but identifies clearly the boundaries of every part of a document. A boundary can be a new chapter, a new paragraph (text), or a new reference.

Note: A document is anything that can be logically structured with content and containers. An XML document is similar to the desktop icons "folder" and "trash can."

For this to happen, a user must provide a document type definition (DTD) that declares each of the permitted elements, attributes, entities and the relationships between elements and entities. These declarations define the boundaries.

8. How can predefined markup tags be used?

To use a set of predefined markup tags, a user needs to know how the markup tags are delimited from normal text and in which order the various elements should be used.

An XML parser can provide a list of the elements that are valid at each point in the document. Also it should be able to add automatically the required delimiters to the name to produce a markup tag. For example, say a document uses HTML markup and only uses the tag <p>; the parser should note the requirement for the </p> because XML requires both a start-tag and an end-tag.

9. What are the standard XML tags (markup)?

XML does not have a predefined set of tags, like the type defined for HTML, that can be used to mark up documents.

XML is a markup language that can pass information about a document's components from one computer system to another computer system using a DTD.

10. How is XML markup denoted?

Elements and their attributes are entered between matched pairs of angle brackets (<...>). Entity references start with an ampersand and end with a semicolon (&...;). XML tag sets are based on a document's logical structure.

What is a DTD?

A document type definition (DTD) defines the role of each element of text in a formal model. When a DTD is used, a parser can establish that each component of the document occurs in a valid place within the interchanged data stream.

An XML DTD enables a computer, that is, a parser, to check the logical structure of a document. A rule of a logical structure is that a second-level element is not entered prior to its associated first-level element.

XML does not require the presence of a DTD. When a DTD is not used, an XML system may assign a default definition for undeclared components of the markup.

Document Logical Structure

Logical structures for XML documents are covered in detail in Section 3 of the Working Recommendation. A logical structure is a data boundary (element) while a physical structure is a data container (entity). The logical structure of an XML document consists of:

■ Declarations
■ Elements
■ Comments
■ Character references

The logical structure of an XML document is indicated by explicit markup known as elements bounded by:

■ Start-tags
■ End-tags
■ Empty-element tags

An important rule is that for every start-tag there must be an end-tag. XML is rigid about this rule as compared to HTML which permits just a start-tag.

Document Physical Structure

Physical structures for XML documents are covered in detail in Section 4 of the Working Recommendation. A physical structure is a data container (entity) while a logical structure is a data boundary (element). The physical structure of an XML document consists of entities.

Entities are storage units that can have content. All are identified by name except the document entity and the external DTD subset. There is only one document entity.

Entities are either parsed or unparsed. A parsed entity's contents are referred to as its replacement text. This text is an integral part of the document. An unparsed entity's contents may or may not be text.

Markup Declarations Overview

This section is a brief definitional section on the key XML declaration types. Later sections in this chapter give examples on how to do these declaration types. Later chapters on developing XML documents for CORBAservices and CORBAfacilities expand on these fundamental ideas or concepts.

Elements

An element is a key component of a document. It is founded in production Rule 1:

```
document ::= prolog element Misc*.
```

Note: Appendix C is a listing of the 89 production rules.

Element is the XML technique for defining start-tags, end-tags, and empty-element tags. While HTML has a fixed set of tags, XML permits a user to define any number of tag sets. There are three key production rules that govern the notion of element. They are as follows:

■ An element (Rule 39) is delimited by a start-tag and end-tag or by an empty-element tag.

■ Content (Rule 43) is text between a start-tag and end-tag.

■ An empty element (Rule 44) is represented by a start-tag followed by an end-tag, or by an empty-element tag.

Attributes

An attribute (Rule 41) associates a name-value pair with an element (Rule 39). An attribute specification appears only within a start-tag or an empty-element tag. The basic syntax for an attribute list is <!ATTLIST ...>.

An attribute-list declaration specifies the name, data type, and default value (if any) of each attribute associated with a given element. An attribute-list declaration may:

■ Define the set of attributes pertaining to a given element type.

■ Establish type constraints for these attributes.

■ Provide default values for attributes.

Note: More technical information on attributes is found in Section 3.3 of the Working Recommendation and Production Rules 52 and 53.

Entities

There are three key entity notions: entity, entity declaration, and entity reference. An *entity* is any data that can be treated as a unit. An *entity declaration* is governed by Production Rules 70-74. An *entity reference* is governed by Production Rule 67. It signifies that a copy of the entity is to be included at this point.

Notations

Notations identify by name the:

■ Format of unparsed entities.

■ Format of elements that bear a notation attribute.

■ Application to which a processing instruction is addressed.

Notation declarations provide a name for the notation, for use in entity and attribute-list declarations and in attribute specifications, and an external identifier for the notation which may allow an XML processor or its client application to locate a helper application capable of processing data in the given notation. Notation declarations are governed by Production Rules 82 and 83.

Conditional Sections

Conditional sections are portions of the DTD external subset, which are included in or excluded from the DTD's logical structure based on the keyword, which governs them. These sections are governed by Production Rules 61-65.

Processing Instructions

A processing instruction (PI) allows a document to give instructions for one or more applications. A PI can identify the version of XML being used, the way in which it is encoded, and whether it references other files or not.

Developing a Model DTD

This section gives a series of steps for developing a model DTD. An e-mail document type is used as the example. This process is expanded in other chapters where DTDs are developed for CORBA.

After the first section below the created DTD structure is reintroduced after each discussed declaration. Declarations are not necessarily developed as they are given in the DTD. While this may appear to be redundant, it is perhaps better than doing one complete DTD at the chapter's end.

Developing an E-mail's Logical Structure

The first step in designing a document type is to frame the structure for a logical and practical example. In a database document type, one would only need to lay out one record structure unless there are is variation. The following markup has the basic logical document structure (components) of an e-mail document type.

Note: An e-mail document type is a variation of two other document types: a memo and a letter.

```
<!- - e-mail is the root element - ->
<email>
<!- - Sender's e-mail address has defined attributes - ->
<sender>jcaesar@mail.mercury.com</sender>
<!- - a variation on month day year - ->
<!- - Day name, dd/mm/yy usual format - ->
<date>15 Mar 44 BC</date>
<!- - to could be defined to have first and last names - ->
<to>Senators</to>
<!- - could be free form or formalized - ->
<from>Julius Caesar</from>
<!- - carbon copy is an optional element - ->
<cc>W. Shakespeare</cc>
<!- - optional with parsed data - ->
<subject>Attendance</subject>
<!- - could have more than one paragraph - ->
```

```
<text>I will arrive at your gathering at Theater of Pompey in time for
lunch.</text>
</email>
```

Note: The comments <!- - ... - -> reflect design considerations. Also note the use of pairs of start-tags and end-tags (logical elements).

Developing the Tag Sets for an E-mail Document Type

One must create a document type definition (DTD) to define tag sets. The DTD formally identifies the relationships among the various elements that form a document. For a simple email model the XML DTD might be:

```
<!DOCTYPE email [
<!ELEMENT email      (date, to, from, cc?, subject?, text+) >
<!ELEMENT date       (#PCDATA) >
<!ELEMENT to         (#PCDATA) >
<!ELEMENT from       (#PCDATA) >
<!ELEMENT cc         (#PCDATA) >
<!ELEMENT subject    (#PCDATA) >
<!ELEMENT text       (#PCDATA) >
]>
```

This model tells the parser that an email consists of a sequence of header elements: <date>, <to>, <from>, and, optionally <cc> and <subject>. They are to be followed by the contents of the email. There must be at least one paragraph present (indicated by the + after text). In this example, the email's element components have been defined containing parsed character data (#PCDATA), that is, data that has been checked to ensure that it contains no unrecognized markup strings.

Note: For text, one could use p or para for paragraph.

Handling Element Variability

Where the position of an element in the model is variable, the element can be defined as part of a repeatable choice of elements. For example, the model definition for the <text> element could be modified to allow references to citations to books (in a Web environment read this as Uniform Resource Locators (URLs)) or references to figures to be located

anywhere in a paragraph. The element could take this form with two
added element attributes defined:

```
<!ELEMENT text (#PCDATA|citation|figref)+ >
<!- - citation could read url - ->
<!ELEMENT citation (#PCDATA) >
<!ELEMENT figref (#PCDATA) >
```

Note: The preceding example is given to extend the notion of an e-mail.

Developing an Empty-Element Tag

When there is the requirement for a placeholder, an element that does not
require any content, then an empty-element tag is used. No end-tag is
required.

For example, <image/> is a type of empty element that acts as a placeholder for a figure's illustration. There can also be an optional <caption>
element that identifies any text associated with the image. A <figure>
can be defined of consisting of these two elements: <image/> and <cap-
tion>.

The following element declarations extend the email model to include
figures:

```
<!ELEMENT email   (date, to, from, cc?, subject?, (text|figure)+ >
<!- - header information given in an previous example - ->
<!ELEMENT figure  (image, caption?) >
<!ELEMENT image EMPTY >
<!ELEMENT caption (#PCDATA) >
```

Note: Text or a figure can appear one or more times.

Defining an Element's Attributes

Where elements can have variable forms or need to be linked together,
they can be given suitable attributes to specify the properties to be
applied to them.

For example, it might be decided that the <text> field of email could
optionally be printed in bold, italic, or normal. An attribute-list declara-
tion might be: <!ATTLIST text form (bold|italic|normal) "normal" >.

This declaration tells the parser that the <text> start-tag can be amended to read <text form="bold"> or <text form="italic"> if a variant text justification is required. If no such change is stated, the application is to use the default value, that is, <text form="normal">.

Creating a Unique Identifier Attribute

This provides a cross-reference among locations in a document. It ensures that a unique identifier is assigned to an element such as each figure by adding an attribute-list declaration of the following form to the DTD:

```
<!ATTLIST figure id ID #REQUIRED >
```

This declaration tells the parser that each <figure> element entered must have a unique identifier within the start-tag, for example, <figure id="figIX"> rather than <figure>.

Incorporating Standard Text Elements

An example of standard text is boilerplate. For example, Caesar desired to give the appearance of personalizing his email. A boilerplate paragraph could be included as a greeting to the senator's family, such as "I wish all is going well with your household."

Commonly used text can be declared within the DTD as a text entity. A text entity definition could take the form:

```
<!ENTITY mygreeting "I wish all is going well with your household." >
```

Once such a declaration is made in the DTD a user can use an entity reference of the form &mygreeting; in place of the full greeting. Only the declaration in the DTD needs to be changed if Caesar decides to pen a new greeting such as "I came, I saw, I conquered."

Incorporating Non-Standard Text Elements

Non-standard text is text that has characters that are not a part of the standard character set. For example, Caesar wants to include a statement in Greek in his email. The important thing for Caesar to remember here is that the reader has to have an output device (printer or scribe) that handles the character set.

```
<?xml version "1.0" encoding="UTF-16">
```

Note: Greek glyphs (characters) are found in the Unicode Standard 2.1
U+0370 to U+03FF.

Using Text from Any Location

Text stored in another file can also be incorporated into the email using
an entity reference. In this case the entity declaration in the DTD identifies the location of the file containing the text to be referenced:

```
<!ENTITY chapXXI SYSTEM "http://www.JGCaesar.gov/law/volIII/
        chapXXI.xml" >
```

The entity reference &chapXXI; shows where the file is to be added.

Note: Another way to state this entity declaration is:

```
<!ENTITY chap21 SYSTEM "http://www.JGCaesar.gov/law/vol3/chap21.xml" >
```

Declaring a Special Non-Standard Character

Non-standard characters such as umlaut, accents (acute, grave, and cir-
cumflex), and tilde can be declared to show how the characters can be
generated. A typical entry might read:

```
<!ENTITY atilde CDATA "&#227;" >
```

When the string ã is encountered in the text, the parser replaces it
with the code whose decimal value is 227. A hexadecimal equivalent can
be used to do the same thing, ã.

Handling Illustrations

XML has many techniques for handling non-standard document elements.
Where the coding scheme of an element of the file such as an illustration
differs from that used for normal text, the contents of the element can be
treated as an entity with a special notation:

```
<!ENTITY figXIV SYSTEM "http://www.JGCaesar.gov/law/volIII/figures/
        figXIV" NDATA gif >
```

One could also write this entity another way:

```
<!ENTITY fig14 SYSTEM "http://www.JGCaesar.gov/law/vol3/figures/
        fig14" NDATA gif >
```

Details of the relevant notation can be defined as an attribute of an element:

```
<!ATTLIST graphic
        source  %URL;    #REQUIRED
        type    NOTATION (GIF|PNG|JPEG) "JPEG" >
```

To position the figure in the text, a user either enters an entity reference such as &figXIV; (&fig14;) or an empty element such as:

```
<graphic source="http://www.JGCaesar.gov/figures/figXIV.gif"
        type="GIF"/>
```

There also needs to be a notation declaration that tells the application what to do with the unparsed data that is contained in the referenced file. The application's call format might be:

```
<!NOTATION GIF SYSTEM "c:\windows\system\gif.dll" >
```

Handling Different Types of Output

When the text output is on a line-by-line basis, such as computer code, it can be flagged as a special type of parsed character data by addition of a special reserved attribute, xml:space, to the element declaration:

```
<!ELEMENT code (#PCDATA) >
<!ATTLIST code xml:space (default|preserve) #FIXED "preserve" >
```

This declaration preserves the line breaks rather than using the default of replacing line breaks by spaces before justifying the contents of the element.

Developing a Processing Instruction

A processing instruction (PI) allows a document to give instructions for one or more applications. A processing instruction can identify the version of XML being used, the way in which it is encoded, and whether it references other files or not:

```
<?xml version="1.0" encoding="UTF-16" standalone="no">
```

The first part of this PI is only stated if the XML markup adheres to the XML Recommendation. The second part of this PI refers to the type of text format used. In this example it is 16-bit UCS (Universal Multiple-Octet Coded Character Set) Transformation Format. The third part of this PI indicates that there may be external markup declarations.

Developing a Document Type Declaration

A document type declaration should not be confused with a document type definition. A document type declaration either contains the formal markup declarations in its internal subset (between square brackets) or references a file containing the relevant markup declarations (the external subset):

```
<!DOCTYPE email SYSTEM "http://www.JGCaesar.gov/dtds/email.dtd">
```

Role of the Processor

What a processor (parser) should do or not do is defined in the conformance section of the Recommendation (Section 5). Appendix D of this book is a list of the well-formedness constraints a parser must follow. Also in the same appendix is a list of the validity constraints that apply to all valid documents. Throughout the Recommendation are further extension of the implications of the production rules. These extensions include in their wording either "for compatibility" or "for interoperability."

Note: These constraints and rule extensions are discussed throughout this book where it is appropriate.

In doing one's XML design of a document, one should verify that the markup adheres to the well-formedness constraints. The consequence is fatal. Failure to comply with the validity constraints gives unpredictable results. The results could be a sneeze or pneumonia.

There are many options as to the selection of parsers. For the many designers that may be working with Internet Explorer 4.0 there are least two XML parsers by Microsoft:

- The C++ parser is non-validating. (This parser comes with IE 4.0.)
- The Java parser is for application developers.

Note: In Internet Explorer 5.0 there is the capability to use XML to write embedded "data islands" within HTML pages.

Chapter 4

Document Object Model Overview

This chapter looks at one of the newest of the Web document and object-oriented technologies. It is defined in the Document Object Model (DOM) Level 1 Specification, Version 1.0, W3C Recommendation, October 1, 1998. Only Section 1 of the Specification is discussed here because it is concerned with XML. Section 2 of the Specification covers the specifics of the HTML component of the DOM.

The URLs for this specification are:

http://www.w3.org/TR/1998/REC-DOM-Level-1-19981001
http://www.w3.org/TR/1998/REC-DOM-Level-1-19981001/DOM.ps
http://www.w3.org/TR/1998/REC-DOM-Level-1-19981001/DOM.pdf
http://www.w3.org/TR/1998/REC-DOM-Level-1-19981001/DOM.tgz
http://www.w3.org/TR/1998/REC-DOM-Level-1-19981001/DOM.zip
http://www.w3.org/TR/1998/REC-DOM-Level-1-19981001/DOM.txt

Note: The Specification does carry this copyright, "Copyright © World Wide Web Consortium, (Massachusetts Institute of Technology, Institut National de Recherche en Informatique et en Automatique, Keio University). All Rights Reserved."

DOM is important to the conceptual idea of an object-oriented network paradigm (CORBA), to the use of object-oriented languages on the Web, and to the use of XML as an object-oriented markup language or a Web document structure defining language.

Why is knowledge of the DOM important to a developer of XML applications? The DOM permits the developer to view conceptually an XML document as a holder of data. This means an XML document can be considered an object within the CORBA paradigm.

This chapter focuses on:

■ Highlighting the key goals of DOM.

■ Showing some of the possible relationships among DOM, XML, and CORBA.

■ Giving synopses of the XML node interfaces with notes on Java when appropriate.

Note: See the end of the chapter for a *very* simple DOM scenario that includes Java coding, an XML DTD, XML markup, and DOM output.

DOM Defined

The Document Object Model is a *model* by which a Web *document* that contains *objects*, such as elements, can be manipulated. This means one is able to add, change, or delete an element or its attribute in a valid document. There are also the capabilities to get a list of all the elements (the tags rather than the content), such as <para> in the document, and to find all the attributes of a given element.

This means that Level 1 of the DOM allows manipulation of the content in that document. It also allows navigation around an XML document. The goals of Level 2 (publishing date 1999) are to allow manipulation of the Cascading Style Sheets (CSS) attached to an XML document to have an event model and to include enhanced query capabilities.

The Document Object Model is not an object model in the same manner as the Component Object Model (COM). The DOM is a set of interfaces and objects designed for managing XML documents. There is an object model because the DOM identifies:

■ Interfaces and objects that represent and manipulate a document.

■ Interfaces and objects that have the semantics to handle both behavior and attributes.

■ Interface and object relationships and collaborations.

More precisely, the DOM is not:

■ A binary specification

■ A set of data structures

■ A technique of persisting objects to XML

■ A semantic set of definitions for XML

■ A competitor to the Component Object Model (COM)

The DOM is a programming object model that comes from object-oriented design. The Specification interfaces are defined as objects. This implicit data model does <u>not</u> mean that this model has to be used for any interface implementation.

The DOM may be implemented using language-independent systems such as CORBA or COM. CORBA and COM specify interfaces and objects. The DOM may also be implemented using language-specific bindings like the Java or ECMAScript bindings (EMCA-262).

Note: See the latest DOM Specification on the Web for details on these binding implementations.

DOM Specification Abstract

This specification defines the logical structure of XML documents. Manipulation (adding, changing, deleting, and navigating) has been designed for language-neutral and platform-neutral interfaces. A standard set of objects (one each for XML and HTML) represents these document types that provide a model for combining objects and a standard interface for accessing and manipulating them.

More specifically, the DOM Specification defines an application programming interface for XML and HTML. It provides a low-level set of fundamental interfaces that can represent any structured document. It also defines extended interfaces for representing an XML document.

DOM's Language Neutrality

DOM itself is language-neutral. The language to use is dependent upon a number of situations:

■ Application used
■ Browser used (JScript or JavaScript as examples)
■ CSS style sheets required
■ Drivers used such as ODBC
■ Editor used
■ Interface goals defined

DOM Interface

The Object Management Group Interface Definition Language (OMG IDL) was selected as the DOM interface. OMG IDL specifies language and implementation-neutral interfaces. However, the selection of OMG IDL by the DOM Working Group does <u>not</u> imply a requirement to use a specific object binding run time.

Various other IDLs could be used. It is expected by the time you read this book that the DOM can be implemented using CORBA, COM, or Java

Virtual Machine run-time bindings or bindings to various programming languages.

Check the latest version of the Specification to see how the DOM Working Group has specified bindings for Java and ECMAScript (the standardization of JavaScript/JScript by the European Computer Manufacturer's Association (ECMA) defined in ECMA-262). The bindings should be located in one or more appendices to the Specification.

The DOM Specification does <u>not</u> define any methods related to memory management such as releasing an object. This is because the way one deals with memory is language specific. Any memory management method required by a particular language needs to be specified in that language binding.

DOM and Style Sheets

A goal of the DOM Specification Level 2 is to specify a way to manipulate and change Cascading Style Sheets (CSS). There should also be core functionality that may be applicable to other style sheet languages. It is not a goal of Level 2 to specify a similar interface to Extensible Stylesheet Language (XSL).

Entities

There are no objects representing entities in the fundamental DOM interfaces. Numeric character references and predefined entities references in XML are replaced by the single character that makes up the entity's replacement. For example, in:

```
<para>Two famous lovers are Julius &amp; Cleopatra.</para>
```

The "&" is replaced by the character "&", and the text in the <para> element forms a single continuous sequence of characters.

Note: The representations of both internal and external entities are defined within the extended XML interfaces of the DOM.

When a DOM representation of an XML document is serialized, an application needs to check each character in text data to see if it needs to be escaped using a numeric or a predefined entity. Failing to do so could result in validity failure.

DOM Interfaces

The DOM specifies interfaces that may be used to manage XML documents. These interfaces are abstractions, similar to "abstract base classes" in C++. They specify how to access and manipulate an application's internal representation of a document. Any DOM application that adheres to the specified interfaces can maintain documents in any convenient representation. The DOM is designed to avoid implementation dependencies because an existing program may use the DOM interfaces to access software written prior to the existence of the DOM Specification.

The DOM Structure Model Hierarchy

The DOM presents documents as a hierarchy of nodal objects that also implement other, more specialized interfaces. In Java these interfaces are classes. Some root nodes may have children, while others do not. The node types are as follows:

■ *Document*: Element (one permitted), ProcessingInstruction, Comment, DocumentType

■ *DocumentFragment*: Element, ProcessingInstruction, Comment, Text, CDATASection, Entity Reference

■ *DocumentType*: no children

■ *EntityReference*: Element, ProcessingInstruction, Comment, Text, CDATASection, EntityReference

■ *Element*: Element, Text, Comment, ProcessingInstruction, CDATASection, EntityReference

■ *Attr*: Text, EntityReference

■ *ProcessingInstruction*: no children

■ *Comment*: no children

■ *Text*: no children

■ *CDATASection*: no children

■ *Entity*: Element, ProcessingInstruction, Comment, Text, CDATASection, EntityReference

■ *Notation*: no children

Note: The interface hierarchy is contained in the Java org.w3c.dom package.

The interface hierarchy is as follows:

- DOMImplementation
- NamedNodeMap
- NodeList
- Node
  - ❏ Attr
  - ❏ CharacterData
    - ● Comment
    - ● Text
      - ○ CDATASection
  - ❏ DocumentFragment
  - ❏ Document
  - ❏ DocumentType
  - ❏ Element
  - ❏ Entity
  - ❏ EntityReference
  - ❏ Notation
  - ❏ ProcessingInstruction

Note: The interface synopses are discussed as listed in the hierarchy.

NamedNodeMap Interface Synopsis

Objects implementing the NamedNodeMap interface are used to represent collections of nodes that can be accessed by name. NamedNodeMaps are not maintained in any particular order. However, NamedNodeMap may also be accessed by an ordinal index, but this is simply to allow convenient enumeration of its contents.

> **Note:** In Java, a NamedNodeMap is a subclass of type Node. It represents a generic non-editable list of data objects.

Node Interface Synopsis

The Node interface is the primary data type for the entire Document Object Model. It represents a single node in the document tree.

> **Note:** In Java, a Node interface is a Node base class. This class is a fundamental run-time data container. It has a tree structure arrangement. This class includes class constants for:
>
> ■ Document
> ■ Element
> ■ Attribute
> ■ Text
> ■ PI
> ■ Comment

Attr Interface Synopsis

The Attr interface represents an attribute in an Element object. Typically the allowable values for the attribute are defined in a document type definition (DTD).

The DOM views attributes as properties of elements rather than having a separate identity from associated elements. This may make it more efficient to implement such features as default attributes associated with all elements of a given type.

In XML, where the value of an attribute can contain entity references, the child nodes of the Attr node provide a representation in which entity references are not expanded. These child nodes may be either Text or EntityReference nodes. Because the attribute type may be unknown, there are no tokenized attribute values.

> **Note:** The Attribute class holds information about attribute occurrences that appear within an XML document.

CharacterData Interface Synopsis

The CharacterData interface extends Node with a set of attributes and methods for accessing character data in the DOM. No DOM objects correspond directly to CharacterData.

Comment Interface Synopsis

A comment's content is represented by all the characters between the starting '<!--' and ending '-->'. This is the definition of an XML comment.

> **Note:** In Java, the Comment class is a run-time representation of comments.

Text Interface Synopsis

The Text interface represents the textual content (character data in XML) of an Element or Attr. If there is no markup inside an element's content, the text is contained in a single object implementing the Text interface that is the only child of the element. If there is markup, it is parsed into a list of elements and Text nodes that form the list of children of the element.

> **Note:** In Java, the Text class holds data content read in a document instance. The data content is contained in the Java class NodeList.

CDATASection Interface Synopsis

CDATA sections are used to escape blocks of text containing characters that would otherwise be regarded as markup. The only delimiter that is recognized in a CDATA section is the "]]>" string that ends the CDATA section. CDATA sections cannot be nested. The primary purpose is for including material, such as XML fragments, without needing to escape all the delimiters.

Note: The Java class CDATASection represents such information as HTTP headers.

DocumentFragment Interface Synopsis

DocumentFragment enables the extraction of a portion of a document's tree or the creation of a new fragment of a document.

Document Interface Synopsis

The Document interface represents the entire XML document. Conceptually, it is the root of the document tree and provides the primary access to the document's data.

Note: The Document interface is the Java class for the top-level (root) Node of the in-memory, run-time representation of the XML document. It includes the document type declaration associated with a root element of a document instance.

DocumentType Interface Synopsis

Each Document has a doctype attribute whose value is either null or a DocumentType object. The DocumentType interface provides an interface to the list of entities defined for the document.

Element Interface Synopsis

Assume the following XML document:

```
<elementExample id="sample">
  <subelementa/>
  <subelementb><subsubelement/></subelementb>
</elementExample>
```

When represented using DOM, the top node is an Element node for elementExample, which contains two child Element nodes, one for subelementa without a child node and one for subelementb with a child node.

There are methods on the Element interface to retrieve either an Attr object by name or an attribute value by name. In XML, where an attribute

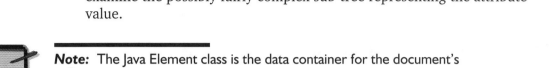

value may contain entity references, an Attr object should be retrieved to examine the possibly fairly complex sub-tree representing the attribute value.

Note: The Java Element class is the data container for the document's elements. The information includes such things as an element's tag set name and its attributes.

Entity Interface Synopsis

This interface represents an entity, either parsed or unparsed, in an XML document. Notice that this interface models the entity, not the entity declaration.

EntityReference Interface Synopsis

EntityReference objects may be inserted into the structure model when an entity reference is in the source document or when the user wishes to insert an entity reference.

Note: Character references and predefined entities references are expanded by the XML processor so that characters are represented by their Unicode equivalent rather than by an entity reference.

Notation Interface Synopsis

This interface represents a notation declared in the document type definition (DTD). A notation either declares by name the format of an unparsed entity or is used for formal declaration of Processing Instruction targets.

Note: The DOM does not support editing Notation nodes.

ProcessingInstruction Interface Synopsis

The ProcessingInstruction interface represents a "processing instruction." A PI is used in XML as a way to keep processor-specific information in the text of the document.

Note: In Java, the Processing Instruction (PI) class is a run-time representation of PIs.

DOM Terms and Definitions

Some of the term definitions used in the DOM Specification were borrowed or modified from similar definitions in other W3C or standards documents. Below are just a few of the key definitions as defined in the Specification that may be directly relevant to a XML document's logical structure.

Ancestor An ancestor node of any node A is any node above A in a tree model of a document, where "above" means "toward the root."

Child A child is an immediate descendant node of a node.

Content model The content model is a simple grammar governing the allowed types of the child elements and the order in which they appear.

Context A context specifies an access pattern (or path), a set of interfaces that gives a way to interact with a model.

Cooked model A model for a document that represents a document after it has been manipulated in some way. For example, any combination of any of the following transformations would create a cooked model:

1. Expansion of internal text entities
2. Expansion of external entities
3. Model augmentation with style-specified generated text
4. Execution of style-specified reordering
5. Execution of scripts

Note: A browser might only be able to provide access to a cooked model, while an editor might provide access to a cooked model or the initial structure model (also known as the uncooked model) for a document.

Cursor	A cursor is an object representation of a node. It may possess information about context and the path traversed to reach the node.
Data model	A data model is a collection of descriptions of data structures and their contained fields, together with the operations or functions that manipulate them.
Descendant	A descendant node of any node A is any node below A in a tree model of a document, where "below" means "away from the root."
Element	Each document contains one or more elements, the boundaries of which are either delimited by start-tags and end-tags or, for empty elements, by an empty-element tag. Each element has a type, identified by name, and may have a set of attributes. Each attribute has a name and a value.
Equivalence	Two nodes are equivalent if they have the same node type and node name. Also, if the nodes contain data, that must be the same. If the nodes have attributes, then a collection of attribute names must be the same and the attributes corresponding by name must be equivalent as nodes.
Inheritance	In object-oriented programming, the ability to create new classes (or interfaces) that contain all the methods and properties of another class (or interface), plus additional methods and properties.
Initial structure model	This model represents the document before it has been modified by entity expansions, generated text, style-specified reordering, or the execution of scripts. It is also known as the raw structure model or the uncooked model.

Interface	An interface is a declaration of a set of methods with no information given about their implementation. In object systems that support interfaces and inheritance, interfaces can usually inherit from one another.
Language binding	A programming language binding for an IDL specification is an implementation of the interfaces in the specification for the given language.
Method	A method is an operation or function that is associated with an object and is allowed to manipulate the object's data.
Model	A model is the actual data representation for the information at hand.
Object model	An object model is a collection of descriptions of classes or interfaces, together with their member data, member functions, and class-static operations.
Parent	A parent is an immediate ancestor node of a node.
Root node	The root node is the unique node that is not a child of any other node. All other nodes are children or other descendants of the root node.
Sibling	Two nodes are siblings if they have the same parent node.
String comparison	When string matching is required, it is to occur as though the comparison were between two sequences of code points from the Unicode 2.0 Standard.
Tag valid document	A document is tag valid if all start-tags and end-tags are properly balanced and nested.
Type valid document	A document is type valid if it conforms to an explicit DTD.
Uncooked model	See initial structure model.
Well-formed document	A document is well-formed if it is tag valid and entities are limited to single elements (i.e., single sub-trees).

Specification References

XML: W3C (World Wide Web Consortium) Extensible Markup Language (XML) 1.0. **http://www.w3.org/TR/REC-xml**.

HTML 4.0: W3C (World Wide Web Consortium) HTML 4.0 Specification. **http://www.w3.org/TR/REC-html40**.

Unicode: The Unicode Consortium. The Unicode Standard, Version 2.0. Reading, Mass.: Addison-Wesley Developers Press, 1996.

CORBA: OMG (Object Management Group) The Common Object Request Broker: Architecture and Specification. **http://www.omg.org/corba/cor-biiop.htm**

Java: Sun. The Java Language Specification. **http://java.sun.com/docs/books/jls/**

ECMAScript: ECMA (European Computer Manufacturers Association) ECMAScript Language Specification. **http://www.ecma.ch/stand/ECMA-262.htm**

Sample DOM Scenario

This scenario consists of four interrelated parts:

- Java code
- XML DTD
- XML Markup
- DOM Output

DOM Java Sample

This sample produces the DOM output sample, BksXML.dom, below. XML for Java includes a com.ibm.xml.parser.Parser class that can simulate an XML parser that can parse an XML document and generate a DOM node tree. Also Java has an interface hierarchy org.w3c.dom package. This sample uses inputs BksXML.dtd and BksXML.xml.

```
import com.ibm.xml.parser.*;
import org.w3c.dom.*;

import java.io.*;
```

```
public class BksXML  {

    public static void main(String[] argv) {
        try  {
            if  (argv.length != 1)   {
                System.out.println("Usage: java BksXML " +
                                        "<document>");
                System.exit(0);
            }

            String fn = argv[0];
            InputStream is = new FileInputStream(fn);

            Parser ps = new Parser(fn);
            Document doc = ps.readStream(is);
            System.out.println("Start document");

            Element el = doc.getDocumentElement();
            printElement(el);

            System.out.println("End document");
        }  catch (Exception e)  {
            e.printStackTrace();
        }
    }
}

public static void printElement(Element el) {
    String en = el.getTagName();
    System.out.println("Start element: " + en);

    NodeIterator ni = el.getAttributes();
    Node n = ni.toNextNode();
    while (n != null) {
        Attribute a = (Attribute) n;
        System.out.println("Attribute: " + a.getName() + "=" +
            ' " ' + a.toString() + ' " ');

        n = ni.toNextNode();
    }

    if (el.hasChildNodes())  {
        ni = el.getChildNodes();
```

```
                    n = ni.toNextNode();
                    while (n != null) {

                    int nt = n.getNodeType();
                    if (nt == Node.Element) {
                        Element e = (Element) n;
                        System.out.println("End Element: " + e);
                    } else if (nt == Node.TEXT)  {
                        TEXT t = (Text) n;
                      System.out.println("Text: " + ' " ' + t.getData() + ' " ');
                    }

                    n = ni.toNextNode();
                }
            }

        System.out.println("End element: " + en);
    }


}
```

DOM XML DTD Sample

This document type definition (DTD) defines the markup tag sets (elements) for the XML encoding below. It is also one of the inputs for the Java application above. The other input is the XML encoding in the following section.

```
<?xml version="1.0" encoding="UTF-16" ?>
<!-- BksXML.dtd  -->
<!- - May have multiple occurences of title, author, and
        description - ->
<ELEMENT BksXML (Title*, Author*, Description*)>

<!ELEMENT Title EMPTY>
<!ATTLIST Title name CDATA #REQUIRED>

<!ELEMENT Author EMPTY>
<!ATTLIST Author Lname CDATA #REQUIRED
                 Fname CDATA #REQUIRED>

<!ELEMENT Description EMPTY>
```

```
<!ATTLIST Description pubr CDATA #REQUIRED
                      pdate CDATA #IMPLIED
                      pgno CDATA #IMPLIED
                      review CDATA #IMPLIED>
```

DOM XML Markup Sample

This sample uses the above DTD. It is also the second input for the above Java application, BksXML.java, the other input being BksXML.dtd. This sample only uses three books and only the first author listed when there is more than one to keep the example simple. Each of these books has established a knowledge niche different from this book and from each other.

```
<?xml version="1.0" ?>
<!-- BksXML.xml -->

<!DOCTYPE BksXML SYSTEM "BksXML.dtd"> [

<BksXML>

<Title name="The XML Handbook"/>
<Title name="Presenting XML"/>
<Title name="Client/Server Data Access with Java and XML"/>

<Author Lname="Goldfarb" Fname="Charles"/>
<Author Lname="Light" Fname="Richard"/>
<Author Lname="Chang" Fname="Dan"/>

<Description pubr="Prentice Hall" pdate="1998"/>
<Description pubr="Sams Net" pgno="414"/>
<Description pubr="John Wiley" review="Covers the client/server
                  paradigm."/>

</BksXML>
]>
```

DOM Output Sample

This is the result of BksXML.java with its inputs of BksXML.dtd and BksXML.xml. If the descriptions in BksXML.xml had been extended, one

could have publication data (pdate), number of pages (pgno), and a
review for each title.

```
Start document
Start element: BksXML
Text: "
"
Start element: Title
Attribute: name="The XML Handbook"
End element: Title
Text: "
"
Start element: Title
Attribute: name="Presenting XML"
End element: Title
Text: "
"
Start element: Title
Attribute: name="Client/Server Data Access with Java and XML"
End element: Title
Text: "
"
Start element: Author
Attribute: Lname="Goldfarb"
Attribute: Fname="Charles"
End element: Author
Text:"
"
Start element: Author
Attribute: Lname="Light"
Attribute: Fname="Richard"
End element: Author
Text:"
"
Start element: Author
Attribute: Lname="Chang"
Attribute: Fname="Dan"
End element: Author
Text:"
"
Start element: Description
Attribute: pubr="Prentice Hall"
Attribute: pdate="1998"
End element: Description
```

```
Text:"
"
Start element: Description
Attribute: pubr="Sams Net"
Attribute: pgno="414"
End element: Description
Text:"
"
Start element: Description
Attribute: pubr="John Wiley"
Attribute: review="Covers the client/server paradigm."
End element: Description
Text:"
"
End element: BksXML
End document
```

Chapter 5

DCAM, IDL, and UML Overviews

Included in This Chapter:

❑ DCAM Overview

❑ Interface Definition Language (IDL) Overview

❑ UML Overview

This chapter gives overviews on three technologies, two for object modeling and the other for describing CORBA interface objects. They have or are going to have an impact on the development of XML applications for CORBA. They are:

■ Distributed Component Architecture Modeling (1999 technology)

■ Interface Definition Language (describes CORBA objects)

■ Unified Modeling Language (models CORBA objects or infrastructure)

Note: In mid-1999 there is not a publicly available prototype of DCAM; however, the concepts that are being developed for this Web technology are important to the general discussion of this book.

A *model* can be considered a small view of a big thing. Actually it can be defined in many ways. There is the toy model such as airplanes or ships. There are general accepted scientific theories that are models of some aspect of perceived reality. When such a theory is disproved, then it also ceases to be a model. Thus, a basic characteristic of a model is its temporariness. Even though a model is temporary, it can, as a visual moment of reality, generate practical solutions to the issues. In this case, the issues are about a CORBA infrastructure.

DCAM Overview

For Distributed Component Architecture Modeling (DCAM), a model can be viewed as an industrial solution framework. Such a model is used as a standard for product integration. A model can be developed to resolve issues for financial, manufacturing, etc. But what is important here is that it can be used to resolve network infrastructure issues particularly with CORBA and the development of XML application. Component can be defined here as an object because in the modeling world objects are referred to as components.

Today's models address high-level operational and functional views of various types of architectures (organizational and in a smaller context these organizations' network infrastructures). These models do not address the information needs for integrating the specific set of interoperable component for any type of infrastructure. Correcting this situation is a key goal of DCAM.

There are many obstacles that DCAM has to overcome. Here is a limited list, but they have significant design and implementation implications:

■ In some cases the model is in the form of a mandate.

■ Rapid rate of technology innovation and change cause most organizations to be ill-equipped to handle either standards compliance or third-party product interoperability.

■ There are a wide variety of industry models.

■ There are a wide variety of standards and related products to fit into the industry models.

■ Time and money needs to be expended.

■ There is a limited knowledge base for IS professionals to use in modeling.

There are a number of events that are driving the DCAM effort, or more importantly the identified need for DCAM. Some of the events or needs are:

■ Advent of the Internet.

■ Cost of downtime.

- Identified new views on software problems and solutions because of the Y2K effort.
- Impact of new technologies and products on network architecture.
- Improving operations and maintenance with a reduced redundant product evaluation and testing process.
- Inadequacies of the client-server paradigm.
- Increase in distributed computing.
- Increased proliferation of standards and vendor initiatives because of the Open Systems concept.
- Interoperability and compatibility between products.
- Introduction of plug and play.
- Maintenance of a system's infrastructure and enhancements with the "daily" commercial technology innovations.
- New tools that document interoperability of products.
- Publication of product interfaces (API).

The Distributed Component Architecture Modeler Prototype in its first phase should include the following features:

- Define API set, versions, support platforms, patches, and product interdependencies.
- Describe services and functions in addressing systems requirements.
- Extend the state-of-the-art in the management of configurations.
- Incorporate "publish and subscribe" technologies to disseminate changes in the repository that impact user domains of interest.
- Manage the inter-relationships of key data points and provide a bidirectional browsing of them.
- Provide a "point and click" Web interface to clearinghouse information.

More simply stated the features are:

- Specification template
- Specification tools
- Test generation tools
- Technology Transfer Kit

Note: The full release for select government, financial, and telecommunications industries is set for the latter part of 1999. The prototype uses Unified Modeling Language (UML).

There are many components of the DCAM effort beyond just the modeling process itself. These components as a part of the Interoperability Clearinghouse (IC) initiative include:

- Analysis Tools—Tools that provide support for a wide range of "views" based on DCAM.
- Component Frameworks—A Web-based component-based architecture modeling tool that allows an industry to combine interoperable products into their domain unique architectures.
- Electronic Forum—A point for dynamic information sharing.
- Information Directory—A Web-based Distributed Component Architecture Modeling (DCAM) tool that enables drill down analyses from architectures to compliant product suites.
- Information Dissemination—Data collection and propagation of the repository though network of IC Partners and Subscribers.
- Information Repository—A Configuration Management type repository application as a back end to the Distributed Component Architecture Modeler to document and communicate findings.
- Interoperability Product Profiles—Product profiles that ensure consistent reporting formats.
- Solution Providers—A logical site for the sharing of information among industries' most critical technology resources: the systems integrators and consultants.
- Standard Templates—Formats and processes for standardization, conformance testing, and interoperability validation.
- Testing Coordination—Cooperative agreements with testing organizations.
- User Coordination (government)—Cooperative agreements (CRADA) with technology-driven agencies.
- User Coordination (industry)—Cooperative agreements with technology-driven commercial industries: finance, insurance, telecommunications, manufacturing, and health care.

- Vendor Coordination—Cooperative agreements with software companies committed to the distributed computing and Internet product markets.

DCAM's evolution requires the inclusion of these features and functions definitions in technology and commercial terms. Some of these features and functions are:

- Allowable solution set definition
- Definition of selected interoperable product suites
- Implemented product suites
- Known third-party product partners.
- Lessons learned from test cases
- Product abstracts for current offerings
- Results of interoperability and conformance test
- Selected infrastructure products
- Selected interoperable product suite definitions
- Standards taxonomies
- Systems testing data
- Target technologies for business applications
- Test results of available test suites and tools

Note: Any network administrator or developer can use this list when considering any major application design.

Interface Definition Language (IDL) Overview

The OMG Interface Definition Language (IDL) describes the interfaces that client objects call and object implementation provides. An IDL interface fully defines an interface and fully specifies each operation's parameters. IDL concepts are mapped to a number of languages such as Java, C++, and Smalltalk.

Note: Java IDL is an Object Request Broker (ORB) provided with JDK 1.2 and complies with the CORBA/IIOP Specification 2.0. The idltojava compiler defines, implements, and accesses CORBA objects from the Java programming language. See the appropriate JDK 1.2 documents for details.

IDL follows the lexical rules of C++. Its grammar is a subset of the proposed ANSI C++ standard. See "The Common Object Request Broker: Architecture and Specification," version 2.2 or later, Chapter 3 for details on IDL at **www.omg.org/corba**.

There is a key principle about IDL that one should be aware of—it is for defining CORBA interfaces and is <u>not</u> for implementing applications. This principle ensures language independence. A server could be written in Java and the client could be written in C++. This adheres to a basic characteristic of CORBA—portability, or the capability to run across a variety of platforms.

IDL definitions can be compared to Java definitions of interfaces or to C++ header files. This is an interface description, not an implementation.

How is language independence achieved? The concept of *language mapping* is used. Language mapping is the process that specifies an IDL construct to another language's construct. The Object Management Group (OMG) has developed a number of language maps for such languages as Java, C, C++, and COBOL. This notion is important because in a given network there may be a variety of legacy programming languages and operating systems. This also gives one the freedom to choose the best language for any given application.

Process for Creating an IDL Server Interface

Since the focus of this book is to make a system administrator aware of issues in the developmental process for an enterprise network using CORBA and not specific solutions, this section is a process overview not an IDL definition solution for a server interface. While the process may be simply stated, one should be experienced in programming and network design.

The process given here is to assist the network administrator in giving directions to the programmers on the team. The steps are few, but the design requires thought. The steps are:

1. Define the IDL server interface.

2. Implement using either the *delegation* or *inheritance* approach.

3. Compile the code to generate *client stubs* and *server skeletons*.

4. Implement the IDL server interface.

5. Compile the server application.

6. Run the server application.

7. Repeat the above steps until step 6 is a success.

Four terms used in steps 2 and 3 need clarification. *Delegation* calls the methods of the implementing class. *Inheritance* passes the methods of the implementing class from the interface class. A *client stub* is a compiled piece of code that makes the interface available to a client. A *server skeleton* is a compiled piece of code that is the "skeleton" or "frame" used for building the server implementation code on the interface.

In a political metaphor, a new president of the United States inherits problems from the prior president, and the new president then delegates his requirements for solutions to his Cabinet. The problems are the president's, while the solutions are the Cabinet's. A client stub is like the social body concerned with the solution. A server skeleton is like the Cabinet Department that has to solve the problem.

Note: An "IDL compiler" is really a translator. It converts IDL source code to the implementation language, Java, C++, etc.

Caution: Before deciding on an approach, you need to understand what the application does. For example, if the application uses legacy code to implement the interface, then the use of the delegation approach is logical. It would not be practical to change the classes in the legacy code to inherit from an IDL compiler generated class.

Process for Creating an IDL Client Interface

It was stated in the previous section that the book's focus is to raise one's awareness to issues in the developmental process for an enterprise network and not offer specific solutions. Local expectations, resources, skills, and the legacy environment determine real solutions. This section is a process overview, not an IDL definition solution for a client interface.

The steps given here as above are to assist the network administrator in giving directions to the programmers on the team. The steps are few; the implementation of the client interfaces should be simpler than the server interfaces. The steps are:

1. Use the client stubs generated in the original compile.
2. Bind the client to a server object.
3. Use the server object interfaces.

UML Overview

Critical to modeling the infrastructure is the Unified Modeling Language (UML). This tool assists in creating an object-oriented design. Rational Software Corporation with a number of partners that include Hewlett-Packard, IBM, Microsoft, and Oracle developed UML for this activity. See Rational Software Corporation's site (**http://www.rational.com/uml/index.jhtml**) for information.

UML seeks to use the best engineering practices for developing large and complex system models. It can be used in both software and non-software environments. This means you can model a client as software and as hardware. It is used for specifying, visualizing, constructing, and documenting a system's infrastructure.

Throughout the design process you have to consider the components of your enterprise network; all of these components make up the infrastructure. The components come in two flavors—concrete and abstract. Knowing what the components are and their places in the enterprise network is key to modeling, determining what tools you need, establishing protocols that implement integration, identifying interconnectivity issues, and establishing the roles of the service and access servers.

Note: The word "component" is used throughout this chapter because most computer literature uses this term based on the client/server paradigm; however, in the context of CORBA and Java internetworking the word "object" is more appropriate.

Concrete components or objects give the structure to the enterprise network. They are things you can see either with your eyes or with graphical user interfaces (management tools).

Abstract components are the functionalism (purposes, utilities, and flows) of the enterprise network. They are things you cannot see either with your eyes or with graphical user interfaces (management tools). The concrete cannot stand alone without the abstract and the abstract cannot stand alone without the concrete. The abstract components are the results of trying to describe the concrete capabilities.

A UML model is like a building blueprint. It aids in system definition, system visualization, and system construction. UML assists you in designing an object-oriented system network.

Besides not being a process, UML is not a programming language. Its name says UML is a modeling language. It is also not a tool interface, but a semantic metamodel. A metamodel is a high-level abstraction.

Chapter 6

Web Interface Definition Language (WIDL)

Included in This Chapter:

- ❏ Overview of WIDL
- ❏ WIDL-SPEC DTD Overview
- ❏ WIDL-MAPPING DTD Overview
- ❏ WIDL Implications for XML and CORBA

Web Interface Definition Language (WIDL) is an important new Web technology for conceptual development of XML applications for CORBA. This technology goes hand-in-hand with the Document Object Model (DOM) and Distributed Component Architecture Modeling (DCAM) technologies. This chapter is detailed since it is important to comprehend WIDL and other IDLs as a foundational requirement for doing modeling with CORBA. The knowledge of XML's place is an integral component of this comprehension.

This chapter looks at the key notions about WIDL version 3.0:

- ■ WIDL overview
- ■ WIDL-SPEC DTD
- ■ WIDL-MAPPING DTD
- ■ WIDL implications for XML and CORBA

This chapter is based on information from

**http://www.transactnet.com/products/toolkit/userguide/refman/widl/
overview.html**

This URL has links to the WIDL Specifications, the WIDL Specification
DTD, the WIDL Mappings, and the WIDL Mapping DTD.

webMethods made a Submission Request to W3C on September 22, 1997
(**http://www.w3c.org/Submission/1997/15/**).

Note: webMethods is a provider of XML-based business-to-business
(B2B) integration solutions and holds copyright to the WIDL
Specification. Check the URL for the latest versions of the
specification and mapping. There are significant differences between
version 2.0 and version 3.0. Because of the dynamics of the
technology, one should expect dynamic changes.

Caution: When quotation marks are used in this chapter, they are a part of
the expected markup. For example, the correct markup is
"SUCCESS," not SUCCESS.

Overview of WIDL

WIDL is an application of XML. It is a metalanguage, a top-level conceptual language that implements a service-based architecture over the
document-based resources of the World Wide Web. This Web technology
uses HTTP for communication among XML and HTML documents (XML
to XML, HTML to HTML, or XML to HTML) by interpreting them as inter-
application messages.

Note: XML and HTML are referenced together in this chapter because of
WIDL's ability to handle XML to HTML communications.

WIDL defines two types of XML documents: a WIDL specification and a
WIDL mapping. These document types conform to XML document type
declarations.

A *WIDL specification* is an XML document that provides an abstract description of an application interface. It names the interface and describes the services that are associated with the interface. Different applications may implement the same specification in different ways. WIDL allows any two applications that conform to the same specification to be interchangeable, so clients need not have knowledge of the details of any application's interface. A WIDL specification provides all of the information required for generating code.

A *WIDL mapping* is an XML document that describes how to map between XML or HTML pages and a WIDL specification. It exposes a Web site or an XML-based application as a set of services. Through a WIDL mapping, a client application may interact with the Web by invoking Web services as if they were implemented as program functions or procedures. WIDL mappings allow applications to interact with the Web without having any knowledge of XML, HTML, or network protocols.

WIDL-SPEC DTD Overview

The elements and attributes of this DTD are described in the five sections that follow the DTD. In this DTD there are the attributes NAME and COMMENT under each element; however, they are <u>not</u> identical. They are unique to that element. The definition of each COMMENT attribute can be phrased in the same manner. The key words in the definition are "of this element."

```
WIDL-SPEC DTD
<!ELEMENT WIDL-SPEC (METHOD | RECORD)+>
<!ATTLIST WIDL-SPEC
  NAME CDATA #REQUIRED
  VERSION CDATA #FIXED "3.0"
  COMMENT CDATA #IMPLIED>

<!ELEMENT METHOD EMPTY>
<!ATTLIST METHOD
  NAME CDATA #REQUIRED
  INPUT CDATA #IMPLIED
  OUTPUT CDATA #IMPLIED
  COMMENT CDATA #IMPLIED>

<!ELEMENT RECORD (VALUE | RECORDREF)+>
<!ATTLIST RECORD
  NAME CDATA #REQUIRED
```

```
  COMMENT CDATA #IMPLIED>

<!ELEMENT VALUE EMPTY>
<!ATTLIST VALUE
  NAME CDATA #REQUIRED
  DIM (0 | 1 | 2)  "0"
  TYPE CDATA "STRING"
  COMMENT CDATA #IMPLIED>

<!ELEMENT RECORDREF EMPTY>
<!ATTLIST RECORDREF
  NAME CDATA #REQUIRED
  DIM (0 | 1 | 2)  "0"
  RECORD CDATA #REQUIRED
  COMMENT CDATA #IMPLIED>
```

WIDL-SPEC Root Element

The root (parent, node) element for a WIDL interface specification is
WIDL-SPEC. The WIDL-SPEC element may contain any number of
METHOD and RECORD sub-elements (signified by the +). The
WIDL-SPEC element has three attributes: NAME, VERSION, and
COMMENT.

NAME

This required attribute establishes an interface
name. An interface name is case sensitive. It
represents either a service name for naming or
directory services. Within an interface name dots
are allowed to delimit a hierarchy of related
interfaces. Example specification names follow:

```
com.mycompany.products.search
com.mycompany.products.purchase
com.mycompany.personnel.address_book
```

Note: webMethods Object Model defines object references. In the
WIDL-MAPPING DTD (the overview is in the next major section),
webMethods can be the value "WOM" in either the CONTENT
attribute of element VALUE or BINDINGREF.

| VERSION | This required attribute must be "3.0". This indicates WIDL 3.0 Specification conformance. |
| COMMENT | This is optional descriptive information of this element. |

METHOD Sub-Element

The METHOD sub-element represents an operation that a client may ask a server to perform. Every method has a name and optionally a set of input and output attributes (parameters). One can also include comments about this sub-element.

NAME	This required attribute establishes a unique method name for the method.
INPUT	This optional attribute names the record that specifies the method's input arguments. The input arguments are the record's fields.
OUTPUT	This optional attribute names the record that specifies the method's output arguments. The output arguments are the record's fields.
COMMENT	This is optional descriptive information of this element.

RECORD Sub-Element

The RECORD sub-element groups and names a collection of fields. It is similar to a Java class that has state variables, but has no methods. A RECORD contains a set of one or more VALUE and RECORDREF elements, each of which is known as a field of the RECORD.

| NAME | This required attribute establishes a unique record name. |
| COMMENT | This is optional descriptive information of this element. |

VALUE Sub-Element

The VALUE empty-element type represents any record field that is not a nested record. A value represents such things as numbers, text, XML, dates, etc. Values are similar to primitive types in most programming languages. Values also represent arrays of these primitive types. The attributes of the VALUE element follow:

NAME	This required attribute establishes a unique record name within a given RECORD.
DIM	This optional attribute defines a field's dimensions.

- "1" indicates a single-dimensional array of strings.

- "2" indicates a two-dimensional array of strings.

- "0" (the default) indicates there is not an array, but a string.

TYPE	This optional attribute identifies the lexical type of the field. Lexical types include integers, floating-point numbers, and strings.

Warning: WIDL Release 3.0 only supports strings. If the TYPE attribute is used it must be "STRING".

COMMENT	This is optional descriptive information of this element.

RECORDREF Sub-Element

The RECORDREF sub-element represents a record that is nested within another record. It is a child of RECORD that is empty. RECORD elements are always immediate children of WIDL-SPEC. The attributes of the RECORDREF sub-element follow:

NAME	This required attribute establishes a unique record name within a given RECORD.
DIM	This optional attribute defines a field's dimensions.

- "1" indicates a single-dimensional array of records.

- "2" indicates a two-dimensional array of records.

- "0" (the default) indicates there is not an array, but a record.

RECORD	This required attribute names the record that nests within the parent RECORD element.
COMMENT	This is optional descriptive information of this element.

WIDL-MAPPING DTD Overview

The elements and their attributes are described in the eight sections that follow the DTD. In this DTD there are the attributes NAME and COMMENT under each element; however, they are <u>not</u> identical. They are unique to that element. The definition of each COMMENT attribute can be phrased in the same manner. The key words in the definition are "of this element."

```
WIDL-MAPPING DTD
<!ELEMENT WIDL-MAPPING (SERVICE | INPUT-BINDING
                        | OUTPUT-BINDING)+>
<!ATTLIST WIDL-MAPPING
  NAME CDATA #REQUIRED
  VERSION CDATA #FIXED "3.0"
  BASEURL CDATA #IMPLIED
  DEFAULT-CONTENT (WOM | CONSTANT) "WOM"
  COMMENT CDATA #IMPLIED>

<!ELEMENT SERVICE EMPTY>
<!ATTLIST SERVICE
  NAME CDATA #REQUIRED
  INPUT CDATA #IMPLIED
  OUTPUT CDATA #IMPLIED
  URL CDATA #REQUIRED
  METHOD (GET | POST) "GET"
  AUTHUSER CDATA #IMPLIED
  AUTHPASS CDATA #IMPLIED
  SOURCE CDATA #IMPLIED
  TIMEOUT CDATA #IMPLIED
  RETRIES CDATA #IMPLIED
  COMMENT CDATA #IMPLIED>

<!ELEMENT INPUT-BINDING (VALUE | BINDINGREF)+>
<!ATTLIST INPUT-BINDING
  NAME CDATA #REQUIRED
  COMMENT CDATA #IMPLIED>
```

```
<!ELEMENT OUTPUT-BINDING (CONDITION | REGION | VALUE
                          | BINDINGREF)+>
<!ATTLIST OUTPUT-BINDING
  NAME CDATA #REQUIRED
  COMMENT CDATA #IMPLIED>

<!ELEMENT CONDITION EMPTY>
<!ATTLIST CONDITION
  TYPE (SUCCESS | FAILURE | RETRY) "SUCCESS"
  REFERENCE CDATA #IMPLIED
  MATCH CDATA #IMPLIED
  WAIT CDATA #IMPLIED
  MASK CDATA #IMPLIED
  REBIND CDATA #IMPLIED
  SERVICE CDATA #IMPLIED
  REASONREF CDATA #IMPLIED
  REASONTEXT CDATA #IMPLIED
  RETRIES CDATA #IMPLIED
  COMMENT CDATA #IMPLIED>

<!ELEMENT REGION EMPTY>
<!ATTLIST REGION
  NAME CDATA #REQUIRED
  START CDATA #REQUIRED
  END CDATA #REQUIRED
  NULLOK CDATA #IMPLIED
  PATTERN CDATA #IMPLIED
  COMMENT CDATA #IMPLIED>

<!ELEMENT VALUE (#PCDATA)>
<!ATTLIST VALUE
  NAME CDATA #REQUIRED
  DIM (0 | 1 | 2) "0"
  TYPE CDATA "STRING"
  CONTENT (WOM | CONSTANT) #IMPLIED
  FORMNAME CDATA #IMPLIED
  USAGE (DEFAULT | HEADER | INTERNAL) "DEFAULT"
  NULLOK (TRUE | FALSE) "FALSE"
  COMMENT CDATA #IMPLIED>

<!ELEMENT BINDINGREF (#PCDATA)>
<!ATTLIST BINDINGREF
  NAME CDATA #REQUIRED
```

```
DIM (0 | 1 | 2) "0"
RECORD CDATA #REQUIRED
CONTENT (WOM | CONSTANT) #IMPLIED
FORMNAME CDATA #IMPLIED
USAGE (DEFAULT | HEADER | INTERNAL) "DEFAULT"
NULLOK (TRUE | FALSE) "FALSE"
COMMENT CDATA #IMPLIED>
```

Note: This DTD, in particular the OUTPUT-BINDING element, was reorganized from the Specification to reflect an XML logical structure.

WIDL-MAPPING Root Element

The root (parent, node) element for WIDL mappings is WIDL-MAPPING. A WIDL mapping is an implementation of a WIDL specification for a particular Web site. A mapping exposes the Web site to programs by making the Web site look like programming language functions rather than XML and HTML documents. These functions are the SERVICE empty-elements of a WIDL mapping document. The WIDL-MAPPING element may contain any number of SERVICE, INPUT-BINDING, and OUTPUT-BINDING elements. The WIDL-MAPPING element has the following attributes:

NAME	This required attribute establishes an interface name. An interface name is case sensitive. It represents either a service name for naming or directory services.
VERSION	This is a required attribute that must have a value of "3.0". This indicates WIDL 3.0 mapping conformance.
BASEURL	This optional attribute is similar to the <BASE HREF=""> statement in HTML. Some of the services within a given mapping may be hosted from the same base URL. If BASEURL is defined, the URL for various services can be defined relative to BASEURL. This feature is useful for replicated sites that can be addressed by changing only the BASEURL, instead of the URL for each service.
DEFAULT-CONTENT	This optional attribute specifies the default content type of VALUE and BINDINGREF elements. The default value is "WOM".

COMMENT   This is optional descriptive information of this
                           element.

SERVICE Empty-Element

The SERVICE empty-element defines an HTTP request, including requests
to CGI scripts or applications that have been integrated through NSAPI,
ISAPI, or other back-end Web server products. Web servers take a set of
input parameters, perform some processing, then return a dynamically
generated XML, HTML, or text document. A WIDL service can also
describe a query within a single document or within a directory structure.

The attributes of the SERVICE empty-element map an abstract service
name into an actual URL, specify the HTTP method to be used to access
the Web server, and designate "bindings" for input and output parameters.
The attributes are:

NAME   This required attribute establishes a unique
                           service name. The service name is case sensitive.
                           It represents either a mapping name for naming
                           or directory services.

INPUT   This optional attribute designates the
                           INPUT-BINDING used to define the input
                           parameters for programs that call the service.
                           The value is the NAME of an INPUT-BINDING
                           found within the same mapping. The value may
                           also take the following form:
                           "<mapping-name>:<binding-name>", where
                           <mapping-name> is the name of another
                           mapping, and where <binding-name> is the
                           name of an INPUT-BINDING within that other
                           mapping. This allows multiple mappings to share
                           the same input parameter definitions. Sharing
                           bindings across multiple mappings is only
                           supported within the B2B Integration Server.

OUTPUT	This optional attribute designates the OUTPUT-BINDING used to define the output parameters for programs that call the service. The value is the NAME of an OUTPUT-BINDING found within the same mapping. The value may also take the following form: "<mapping-name>:<binding-name>", where <mapping-name> is the name of another mapping, and where <binding-name> is the name of an OUTPUT-BINDING within that other mapping. This allows multiple mappings to share the same output parameter definitions. Sharing bindings across multiple mappings is only supported within the B2B Integration Server.
URL	This required attribute specifies the Uniform Resource Locator (URL) for the target document. A service URL can be either a fully qualified URL or a partial URL that is relative to the BASEURL provided as an attribute of the WIDL-MAPPING element.
METHOD	This required attribute specifies the HTTP method used to access the service. The valid values are "GET" (the default) and "POST".
AUTHUSER	This optional attribute establishes the HTTP authentication username.
AUTHPASS	This optional attribute establishes the HTTP authentication password.
SOURCE	This optional attribute sets the HTTP REFERER header variable. Sites can check this variable to ensure that the client originated from a particular page. A mapping may also set the REFERER variable by defining a VALUE parameter within the service's input binding, where the parameter is named "REFERER" and where the USAGE attribute is set to "HEADER". When present, a service's SOURCE attribute always overrides this parameter.
TIMEOUT	This optional attribute is the number of seconds before the service times out.

RETRIES	This optional attribute is the number of retries before failing the service.
COMMENT	This is optional descriptive information of this element.

INPUT-BINDING Element

The INPUT-BINDING element defines the input parameters of a service. This element contains one or more VALUE elements, each of which corresponds to an input parameter of the service. Input-bindings describe the data submitted in an HTTP request, and are similar to the input fields in an HTML form. For static HTML documents, no input fields are required.

NAME	This required attribute identifies the binding for reference by SERVICE elements. No two bindings may have the same name within a given WIDL-MAPPING. Input bindings and output bindings use the same namespace.
COMMENT	This is optional descriptive information of this element.

OUTPUT-BINDING Element

The OUTPUT-BINDING element defines a group of output parameters. A service may specify its output parameters by setting its OUTPUT attribute to the name of an output binding. An output binding may contain parameters that are themselves other output bindings, so that bindings may nest within bindings to form complex output structures.

An output binding sets the values of its parameters by extracting information from an XML or HTML document or from a portion of an XML or HTML document. The process of pulling information out of a document in order to assign parameters is known as *binding*.

When a service's OUTPUT attribute names a binding, each parameter binds against the entire document. When the RECORD attribute of a BINDINGREF element names a binding, each parameter binds against the portion of the document that the BINDINGREF element identifies. By including BINDINGREF parameters within output bindings, one may create structures of nested records. Each record is the result of having applied any output binding to any portion of the document. Also, a given binding might be applied multiple times against multiple portions of the document.

An OUTPUT-BINDING consists of any number of REGION, CONDITION, VALUE and BINDINGREF child elements. The VALUE and BINDINGREF elements define the output binding's parameters. The attributes of OUTPUT-BINDING follow:

NAME	This required attribute identifies the binding for reference by SERVICE and BINDINGREF elements. No two bindings may have the same name within a given WIDL-MAPPING. INPUT-BINDING and OUTPUT-BINDING names belong to the same namespace.
COMMENT	This is optional descriptive information of this element.

CONDITION Sub-Element

The CONDITION empty-element specifies success and failure conditions for the extraction of data to be returned to calling programs in output bindings. Conditions enable branching logic within service definitions. These conditions are used to attempt alternate bindings when initial bindings fail and to initiate service chains, whereby the output variables from one service are passed into the input bindings of a second service.

Conditions also define error messages returned to calling programs when services fail. Any output binding parameter that returns a NULL value causes the entire binding to fail, unless the NULLOK attribute of that parameter has been set to "TRUE". Conditions can catch the success or failure of either a specific object reference or of an entire binding. In the case where a condition initiates a service chain, it is important that all parameters bind properly.

TYPE	This required attribute specifies whether a condition is checking for the "SUCCESS" or the "FAILURE" of a binding attempt. The other attributes of the CONDITION element specify the operation to perform under this condition. Also, TYPE may assume a value of "RETRY" to indicate the response to a server-busy indication. In this case, the condition performs a number of retries

	with a given timeout (TIMEOUT and RETRIES attributes).
REFERENCE	This optional attribute specifies an object reference that extracts data from the XML or HTML document returned as the result of a service invocation. The REFERENCE attribute for conditions is equivalent to the element content of VALUE and BINDINGREF elements.
MATCH	This optional attribute specifies a text pattern that compares the object property referenced by the REFERENCE attribute.
WAIT	This optional attribute is the number of seconds to wait before retrying for document retrieval after a server has returned a "service busy" error. Applies only to conditions of type "RETRY".
MASK	This optional attribute specifies a portion of the text that REASONREF returns. This portion becomes the returned reason string. The syntax of a mask is the same as the syntax defined for masks in object references.

Note: It is not necessary to use this attribute, since the WOM expression found in REASONREF may perform the masking.

REBIND	This optional attribute specifies an alternate output binding. Typically a failure condition indicates the document returned cannot be bound properly. REBIND redirects the binding attempt to another output binding. Rebinding is useful in situations where the documents returned by a service are dependent upon the input criteria that were submitted. The use of REBIND allows a condition to determine the appropriate binding for extracting the desired data.

SERVICE	This optional attribute specifies a service to invoke with the results of an output binding, thus implementing a service chain. The value is the name of a SERVICE found within the same mapping. The value may also take the following form: "<mapping-name>:<service-name>," where <mapping-name> is the name of another mapping, and where <service-name> is the name of a SERVICE within that other mapping. This allows chaining across the services of multiple mappings, but this feature is only supported within the B2B Integration Server.
REASONREF	This optional attribute is an object reference pointing to a value to be returned as an error message when a service fails. A condition cannot contain values for both REASONTEXT and REASONREF.
REASONTEXT	This optional attribute returns the text for an error message when a service fails. A condition cannot contain values for both REASONTEXT and REASONREF.
RETRIES	This optional attribute is the number of times to retry before failing the service. Applies only to conditions of type "RETRY".
COMMENT	This is optional descriptive information of this element.

REGION Sub-Element

The REGION empty-element in an output binding defines targeted sub-regions of a document. Regions are useful in services that return variable arrays of information in structures that can be located between well-known elements of a page.

Note: Regions are critical for poorly designed HTML documents where it is otherwise impossible to differentiate between desired data elements and elements that also match the search criteria.

| NAME | This required attribute specifies a region's name. This name can then be used as the root of an object reference. For instance, a region named "foo" can be used in object references such as: foo.p[0].text. |

Note: The origins of "foo" could be for food, for fool, or for file object-oriented.

START	This optional object reference determines the beginning of a region.
END	This optional object reference determines the termination of a region.
NULLOK	This optional attribute is either "TRUE" or "FALSE". This is the indicator that determines whether it is acceptable for the parameter's object reference to fail to bind. When false, if object reference does not bind, the entire binding fails. CONDITION elements may then be used to handle the failed binding. By default, a failure to bind any parameter fails the entire binding.
PATTERN	This optional attribute defines a pattern of elements to match within a region. A pattern consists of a set of space-delimited element type names. The resulting region consists of these elements. The asterisk matches any number of elements but does <u>not</u> select elements for inclusion in the region.
COMMENT	This is optional descriptive information of this element.

VALUE Sub-Element

The VALUE element represents a string parameter of an input binding or an output binding. As an input parameter it defines the value of an input variable that is submitted to a Web server. As an output parameter it defines how the parameter's value is extracted from the documents that the server returns.

VALUE does not contain any child elements, but the content enclosed between the VALUE start-tag and the VALUE end-tag has significance. An input parameter need not have any content between these tags, in which case only an empty start-tag (such as <VALUE NAME="N1"/>) need be specified. This signifies that the program that calls the service provides the parameter value. When an input parameter does have content, the content represents a string constant that is to be submitted to the server as the value of the input variable. In this case, the program does not provide a value.

An output parameter must have content between the VALUE start-tag and end-tag. The content represents either a constant or an object reference. When it represents a constant, the parameter always returns the content as its value. Constants may use the %% notation for parameter substitution (see the USAGE attribute), so that the parameter's value is a concatenation of constant strings and dynamically assigned parameter values. When the content represents an object reference, the object reference extracts information from the XML or HTML page that the server returns, and the resulting information becomes the value of the parameter.

NAME	This required attribute identifies the parameter to calling programs. No two parameters may have the same name within a given binding. VALUE and BINDINGREF names belong to the same namespace.
DIM	This optional attribute defines a parameter's dimensions.

- ■ "1" indicates a single-dimensional array of strings.
- ■ "2" indicates a two-dimensional array or table of strings.
- ■ "0" (the default) indicates there is not an array, but a string.

TYPE	This optional attribute specifies the data type of the parameter. When present, this parameter must take a value of "STRING".

CONTENT

This optional attribute identifies the type of expression found within the content of the element, where the content is the string that resides between the VALUE start-tag and the VALUE end-tag. The valid values are "WOM" and "CONSTANT". WOM is an abbreviation for webMethods Object Model, which defines object references. If the CONTENT attribute is absent, the value of the attribute assumes the value of the WIDL-MAPPING element's DEFAULT-CONTENT attribute. Input parameters may not have a content type of "WOM".

In addition to the above attributes, input parameters <u>must</u> have the following attribute, FORMNAME:

FORMNAME

This required attribute specifies the variable name to be submitted through the HTTP GET or POST method. The calling program provides the value that is assigned to the variable, unless the CONTENT attribute is set to "CONSTANT", in which case the element's content is submitted as the value.

The FORMNAME attribute allows one to assign meaningful names to obscure form name variables. One may set FORMNAME to the empty string ("") to pass only the value of the input variable and not also a variable name, as required by some Web services.

USAGE

This is an optional attribute. The DEFAULT usage of variables is for specification of input and output parameters. Parameters can pass HEADER information (for example, USER-AGENT or REFERER) in an HTTP request.

One may also reference INTERNAL parameters from within attributes and element content by using the syntax "%<parameter>%". This performs string substitution for string parameters and parameter value assignment otherwise. (The syntax may also be used for non-internal parameters.)

In addition to the common attributes, an output parameter <u>may</u> have the following attribute, NULLOK:

NULLOK   This optional attribute is either "TRUE" or "FALSE". This is the indicator that determines whether it is acceptable for the parameter's object reference to fail to bind. When false, if object reference does not bind, the entire binding fails. CONDITION elements may then be used to handle the failed binding. By default, a failure to bind any parameter fails the entire binding.

COMMENT   This is optional descriptive information of this element.

BINDINGREF Sub-Element

The BINDINGREF element represents a structured record parameter of an output binding. The element serves as a reference to another binding. Each BINDINGREF provides a parameter name and the name of an output binding that the parameter represents. This element provides the mechanism by which bindings are nested within bindings. BINDINGREF is like VALUE in that both are binding parameters.

Each BINDINGREF contains an object reference between the BINDINGREF start-tag and the BINDINGREF end-tag. The object reference identifies one or more portions of an XML or HTML document. If the binding reference's DIM attribute is "0" or not present, the binding reference represents a single instance of another binding, and the object reference identifies a single portion of the document. If the DIM attribute is "1", the binding reference represents an array of bindings, and the object reference represents an array of portions of the document. The multiplicity of the object reference must agree with the dimensionality of the BINDINGREF.

Also, the object reference of a BINDINGREF never specifies the document element and never specifies an object property. Instead, the object reference is always expressed relative to the object reference of the containing OUTPUT-BINDING. For example, "TR[]", "TR[].TD[0]", and "product[]" are all valid BINDINGREF object references, while "doc.TR[]",

"TR[].TD[0].source", and "doc.product[].source" are not valid in binding references. The attributes are:

NAME

This required attribute identifies the parameter to calling programs. To access parameters within the nested binding, the program must refer to those parameters relative to the binding reference's name. No two parameters may have the same name within a given binding. VALUE and BINDINGREF names belong to the same namespace.

DIM

This optional attribute defines a parameter's dimensions.

■ "1" indicates an array of bindings.

■ "2" is not valid.

■ "0" (the default) indicates there is a single binding.

RECORD

This required attribute identifies the output binding that the binding reference is to nest within its parent output binding. The value is the name of an OUTPUT-BINDING found within the same mapping. The value may also take the following form: "<mapping-name>:<binding-name>", where <mapping-name> is the name of another mapping, and where <binding-name> is the name of an OUTPUT-BINDING within that other mapping. This allows multiple mappings to share the same output bindings. Sharing bindings across multiple mappings is only supported within the B2B Integration Server.

CONTENT

This optional attribute identifies the type of expression found within the content of the element, where the content is the string that resides between the BINDINGREF start-tag and the </BINDINGREF> end-tag. When present, the value must be "WOM". WOM is an abbreviation for webMethods Object Model, which defines object references. If the CONTENT attribute is absent, the value of the attribute assumes the value of the WIDL-MAPPING element's DEFAULT-CONTENT attribute.

In addition to the above attributes, input parameters <u>must</u> have the following attribute, FORMNAME:

FORMNAME	This required attribute specifies the variable name to be submitted through the HTTP GET or POST method. The calling program provides the value that is assigned to the variable, unless the CONTENT attribute is set to "CONSTANT", in which case the element's content is submitted as the value.
	The FORMNAME attribute allows one to assign meaningful names to obscure form name variables. One may set FORMNAME to the empty string ("") to pass only the value of the input variable and not also a variable name, as required by some Web services.
USAGE	This is an optional attribute. The DEFAULT usage of variables is for specification of input and output parameters. Parameters can pass HEADER information (for example, USER-AGENT or REFERER) in an HTTP request.
	One may also reference INTERNAL parameters from within attributes and element content by using the syntax "%<parameter>%". This performs string substitution for string parameters and parameter value assignment otherwise. (The syntax may also be used for non-internal parameters.)

In addition to the common attributes, an output parameter <u>may</u> have the following attribute, NULLOK:

NULLOK	This optional attribute is either "TRUE" or "FALSE". This is the indicator that determines whether it is acceptable for the parameter's object reference to fail to bind. When false, if object reference does not bind, the entire binding fails. CONDITION elements may then be used to handle the failed binding. By default, a

| | failure to bind any parameter fails the entire binding. |
| COMMENT | This is optional descriptive information of this element. |

WIDL Implications for XML and CORBA

As is seen in other parts of this book the notion or functionality of an Interface Definition Language (IDL) is not unique. In CORBA the IDL describes the interfaces to CORBA objects in a distributed environment. WIDL from webMethods describes Web resources so a user can automate all XML and HTML documents and forms interactions. WIDL follows the trend to describe data within documents rather than the documents themselves.

The WIDL specification provides an abstract description for an API to services, while the WIDL mapping provides the interactions among XML and HTML documents.

Note: A service is a function that resides behind a Web XML or HTML document such as a Common Gateway Interface (CGI) script. An interface is a collection of services.

WIDL describes the location of services at the highest Web level, URL. The input parameters to be submitted to a service are described in the WIDL-MAPPING root element and its SERVICE element with its METHOD attribute. The output parameters to be returned for a service are described likewise.

XML and WIDL-SPEC Interface

Below is a template example of an XML implementation for a service using WIDL-SPEC. This template can be the basis for developing an interface to a book catalog service.

```
<WIDL-SPEC NAME="com.wordware.books.catalog"  VERSION="3.0">

<METHOD NAME="getbook"
        INPUT="BookList"
        OUTPUT="BookCatalog" />
```

```
<RECORD NAME="Title">
    <VALUE NAME="CORBA Developer's Guide with XML" />
</RECORD
<RECORD NAME="Author">
    <RECORDREF NAME="LastName"
               RECORD="Doss" />
    <RECORDREF NAME="FirstName"
               RECORD="George" />
</RECORD>

</WIDL-SPEC>
```

WIDL is parsed as an XML document. This process extracts relevant data about services declared. To retrieve available services in a given WIDL file, this simple object reference would be used:

```
widl.service[].name
```

Note: Similar object references would be used to retrieve a URL, a service method, and input and output variables.

Condition Handling

Because there is no standard for handling errors for document formats, WIDL's CONDITION is very useful. CONDITION can handle object references that return either meaningless data or null values. A simple CONDITION declaration is:

```
<CONDITION TYPE="FAILURE"
           REFERENCE="doc.xml[0].value"
           MATCH="*error condition*"
           REASONTEXT="error condition" />
```

Note: By using REASONREF, conditions can divert a service to an alternate set of object references for output variables.

Part II

CORBA: Why and What

Included in This Part:

- Chapter 7—CORBA Headlines
- Chapter 8—Essentials of CORBAservices
- Chapter 9—Essentials of CORBAfacilities

Chapter 7

CORBA Headlines

Included in This Chapter:

❑ Headlines on CORBA Objects

❑ Headlines on the ORB

❑ Headlines on CORBA Domains

❑ Headlines on CORBAservices

❑ Headlines on Security Service

❑ Headlines on CORBAfacilities

❑ Basic Designed XML/CORBA DTD

The selection of "headlines" as a part of this chapter's title is important to a discussion of CORBA and XML. A headline in a newspaper is a method of attracting one to read a story; if a good one, it should also be a theme or viewpoint of the story. Consider what you think when you see these headlines:

■ Octuplets born in Houston
■ Storm causes 500 car accidents

Each of these headlines generates a different set of images and emotions. Are the images and emotions correct? Until one knows that the octuplets are human children and not elephants, one might have a different image than is expected. Also, with accidents one might wonder if there were any deaths.

Where does this lead? It seems that we humans are always seeking clarification. When one sees a statement such as "CORBA is a dynamic paradigm that is going to shift a system administrator's view of networking significantly," what images and emotions are generated? Perhaps chaotic images and fearful emotions are generated.

If one considers when one first heard about the client/server paradigm, one might also have the same type of images and emotions. But the key word is image. Just as with the octuplets example, one must clarify CORBA or client/server. It is a given here that one already has experience with the client/server paradigm (a two-sided viewpoint). Actually, we have many two-sided paradigms, and the client/server is a key one for the computer environment. Other associated computer paradigms include:

- Parent/child
- Input/output
- Data/information
- Hardware/software

What fundamentally makes the CORBA paradigm different from the client/server paradigm? There are five basic concepts that make the difference; all else is commentary:

- Common (There is "sameness.")
- Object (There is something "perceptible.")
- Request (There is the act "of asking.")
- Broker (There is the "handler" of the asking.)
- Architecture (There is the "design and structure" for containing the other four.)

XML has a user-defined architecture, the document type definition (DTD). A DTD should be able to handle common objects and requests. In a client/server XML DTD one might have an attribute list of "yes" and "no"; however, in a CORBA XML DTD one might have an attribute list of "yes", "no", and "maybe". The absolute "either-or" dichotomy is less relevant in the CORBA paradigm. An important concept of CORBA is that an object can be accessed by another object and it can also access another object. In other words, a client can be a server, and a server can be a client. An XML DTD can be designed to permit one to define an object either way. Thus, the octuplets in the first headline could be defined as a group, not as a number, in XML markup as:

```
<anmlgrp>octuplets</anmlgrp >
```

```
<hmngrp>octuplets</hmngrp >
<group>octuplets</group>
```

Note: An XML tag set should be meaningful. Here is an example of thinking about design. In a database about animals and humans one could have an element—start-tag, content, end-tag—have the same content but different representations. One could also associate a group with animal or human and not need the other two tag sets.

This chapter is a commentary on the five basic concepts using headlines. It is not an overview. It is not a view of the world from Mt. Olympus or Mt. Sinai. It is not an "essentials" discussion. What one does not know is always the essential need. It is not highlights of CORBA. Lowlights can also be important. This chapter comments on these key areas: CORBA object, the ORB, domains, CORBAservices, the Security Service, and CORBAfacilities. This chapter is primarily concerned with the design or structure of CORBA rather than the how-it-works. It is a search for the components, contents, constituents, ingredients, parts, or widgets of CORBA. In XML terminology or jargon, it is a search for elements, attributes, and entities. The chapter ends with a basic designed XML/CORBA DTD that represents a fundamental design pattern for more complex designed DTDs developed in Part III of this book.

To develop a set of headlines for CORBA one might think of a house. If a realtor was to show you through a house, the type of headlines the realtor would use are:

- "This is the hallway."
- "This is the living room."
- "This is the bedroom."
- "This is 'x'."

One would get images as to what should go in that room or not go in that room. You would not expect to put your bed in the living room. A television might go in both rooms. So a room can be considered in computer jargon as a feature or function, while a bed or television can be considered an attribute. A room can be considered an entity because it holds things. For example, CORBA has COMMON Facilities.

Note: A headline may only give a partial view of reality. It takes the commentary or detailed text to clarify.

Headlines on CORBA Objects

A CORBA object may be consider a foundational abstraction for comprehending this object-oriented paradigm. These headlines are a place to start thinking about an object as an element, an attribute, or an entity; they are not the place to end. Here are 20 random headlines for a CORBA object:

- An object is unique.
- Objects have versions.
- An object contains data.
- An object cannot change type.
- An object can be accessed by name.
- CORBA can handle internationalization.
- Object relationships need to be expressed.
- An object is a discrete software component.
- An object receives messages through the ORB.
- The object model is the object's most abstract form.
- A CORBA object is an interface definition in IDL.
- An object has operations, attributes, and exceptions.
- An object has a state different from any other object.
- "Namespaces" and "object handles" support naming.
- An object instance can be considered a *template* or a *class*.
- A CORBA object is similar to a programming object, but not the same.
- Object distribution is based on a number of areas including location and access.
- CORBA has four objects/interfaces: application, domain, facility, and service.
- Operational performance has a number of objectives including scalability and throughput.
- An object can be invoked through three methods: intraprocess, interprocess, and intermachine.

What can one identify from these headlines about a CORBA object? A key idea is that a CORBA object might be equated to an XML entity because it contains data. (An XML entity is a container.) An object can be identified with a number of attributes such as operational performance and distribution. The places of a CORBA object in an XML DTD are discussed in Chapters 11-14.

Note: The design logic based on the above is that a CORBA object is a container. CORBAservices and CORBAfacilities are CORBA objects; thus they are containers. An XML entity is a container. The root entity or top-level entity is the document entity. A document type is a root entity. A CORBA service or CORBA facility could be equated to a document type.

Headlines on the ORB

CORBA can be viewed in two ways. First, CORBA can be Common Object Request Broker Architecture. This implies an architecture that has a unified environment, sees components as unique, handles the acts of asking, and manipulates the acts of asking. Second, CORBA can be Common ORB Architecture. This view gives a new perspective in which common modifies a unique actor, the Object Request Broker. The actor has architecture in that it has a structure or is a system. These headlines reflect the emphasis on the second view stated here.

The ORB is an abstract bus. Two concrete types of buses are the one that carries passengers and the electrical bus. Bus is an abbreviated form of omnibus, or "vehicle for all." This is a textual way of not drawing a figure that is different between versions of CORBA, but the ORB is the centerpiece of the architecture because all messaging goes through it. An orb can be viewed as a sphere or as a range of activities or influences. The ORB influences everything else in the architecture.

Since a precedent has been established, here are 20 headlines on the ORB:

■ The ORB has objects.
■ An ORB is a type of proxy.
■ An ORB is location transparent.
■ The ORB ID is a string identifier.
■ The ORB conveys messages to objects.
■ ORB is an instance of CORBA, a class.
■ The ORB skeleton interface is proprietary.

- An ORB domain is one implementation instance.
- The ORB handles any CORBA object invocation.
- A client may transparently use any number of ORBs.
- The ORB does <u>not</u> have all the capabilities of a broker.
- The ORB is middleware that interfaces to a set of APIs.
- The ORB is a type of scaling implement or mechanism.
- The ORB is a major component of the OMG Reference Model.
- Any ORB is known by the scope of its *objrefs*, object references.
- The ORB is not an object-oriented remote procedure call (OO RPC).
- The ORB is a communication platform that facilitates object interoperability.
- The interface between an ORB and an object implementation is an object adapter.
- An ORB can provide invocation either by interprocess, intraprocess, or intermachine.
- The ORB interface is a collection of operations that provides common services to clients and servers.

From these headlines one can determine that an ORB is a facilitator of objects and the ORB has a number of functional attributes. One can also determine some of its relationship to other CORBA components. Would you consider an ORB an XML entity?

Headlines on **CORBA** Domains

A simple definition of a CORBA domain is a set of objects for a defined function. This definition of a domain is very close to one in the common language, "a sphere (area) of activity or function." There are a number of domain types including network addressing, network connectivity, reference, and transaction. The OMG is working on specific domain objects such as electronic commerce, manufacturing, and telecommunications.

Domain is looked at in more detail in Chapter 11. Here are 20 headlines related to domain:

- A domain has a common set of rules.
- A domain has transparent distribution.
- A domain can be modeled as an object.
- Naming domains may not need bridging.

- A domain is important to interoperability.
- Domains are connected to each other through bridges.
- In CORBA a domain is a modeling concept.
- A domain has a set of common characteristics.
- A domain can be a member of another domain.
- A concept important to domain is object references.
- The concept domain is a work in progress by the OMG.
- Domains relate through either containment or federation.
- A key word to describe a domain is scope, a meaningful limit.
- A domain boundary needs to be identified by a meaningful identifier.
- There are many domain types (business, language, management, etc.).
- One domain can coexist with another domain through common objects.
- A simple notation of a domain is that it comprises the set of objects of one ORB.
- Two or more domains can be mapped either by mediated bridging or immediate bridging.
- A domain allows system partitioning into components with common characteristics.
- A complex notation of a domain is that it comprises all the ORBs of a service such as networking.

Headlines on CORBAservices

CORBAservices are interfaces that have been standardized by the OMG for use by developers. In theory, this means common usage across platforms and products is possible. In practice, this simply shows to what degree developers have implemented the CORBAservices. More details on CORBAservices are discussed in Chapters 8, 12, and 13. Here are 20 headlines for CORBAservices:

- CORBAservices are inherent to most objects.
- CORBAservices are service-defined interfaces.
- CORBAservices provide for the creation of objects.
- CORBAservices provide for access control of objects.
- CORBAservices address the functions of applications.

- CORBAservices are also referred to as Object Services.
- The Naming Service registers and locates objects by name.
- CORBAservices do not have standardized implementations.
- CORBAservices provide maintenance of object relationships.
- The Property Service enables objects to define sets of properties.
- CORBAservices are a growth area (at least 15 and counting).
- CORBAservices defines conventions for distributed applications.
- The Event Service manages which objects send or receive events.
- The Concurrency Control Service uses locks to manage concurrency.
- CORBAservices are defined through the Interface Definition Language.
- The Persistent Object Service manages objects that persist over a time period.
- The Licensing Service supports three policies: consumer, time, and value mapping.
- The Life Cycle Service facilitates the creating, deleting, copying, and moving of objects.
- The Object Trader Service locates objects in three ways: function, location, and operation name.
- The Security Service handles the basic components of a security policy such as identification and authentication.

What can one learn from these headlines? CORBAservices can be generalized, but the characteristics of a specific service may give more insight. Since this is a very dynamic area, one should adhere to a key programming guideline—be scalable. Implementation is left to the developer, usually read as vendor.

Headlines on Security Service

All services may be equal, but perhaps some are more equal than others. The basic service is the Naming Service; however, from more than a technical view a service that comes quickly to a developer's mind is security. The vision for the Security Service is for it to handle basic components of a security policy. The Security Service is discussed in more detail in Chapter 13. Here are ten Security Service headlines:

- Security Service is a work in progress.
- Security Service has to be enforceable.

- Security Service is fundamentally a security policy.
- Security Service has to reflect business and regulatory requirements.
- Security Service has to be consistent, scalable, portable, and usable.
- Having a Security Service does not mean being able to do more, but less.
- Security Service architecture is based on components rather than implementations.
- Security Service is concerned with functions, mechanisms, services, policies, and threats.
- Security Service architecture is based on a white paper written by security specialists (1994).
- Security Service is important because natural boundaries of protection are blurred in an object-oriented environment.

Headlines on CORBAfacilities

CORBAfacilities are more complex than CORBAservices because of the level of aggregation of the services. CORBAfacilities are optional, while CORBAservices are not. The identified components for CORBAfacilities applications cover a wide spectrum of domains. CORBAfacilities are discussed in more detail in Chapters 9 and 14. Here are ten CORBAfacilities headlines:

- CORBAfacilities use the ORB to communicate.
- CORBAfacilities are also known as Common Facilities.
- CORBAfacilities have been divided into four basic types by the OMG.
- CORBAfacilities can be considered vertical when the applications are generic.
- CORBAfacilities can be considered horizontal when the applications are specific.
- The User Interface Facility encompasses major user interface enablers.
- The development for CORBAfacilities is more dynamic than that for CORBAservices.
- The System Management Facility is difficult to develop even after a lengthy period.
- The Task Management Facility is concerned with the automation and execution of user tasks.

■ The vision for the Information Management Facility is to have a standard set of services to manipulate OMA-based schema.

Basic Designed XML/CORBA DTD

XML uses the document type metaphor to permit one to design anything using the logical and physical structures of a document. So for any application or operational design that includes XML one must have a design comprehension of both a document type and the subject type that is to be metamorphosed (transformed into) as a document. A document type can be many things: a memo, a letter, a textbook, a novel, etc. The subject type of interest here is CORBA.

One could look at CORBA perhaps as either a textbook or a novel. The textbook has a detailed logical structure of chapter number, title, a number of header levels, paragraphs, figures, and ordered and unordered lists. A novel might only have a chapter number and paragraphs. However, each could have more components (elements). Other chapters in this book illustrate how the textbook metaphor can be fully used with CORBA. Here is a very simple example of an XML DTD for CORBA:

```
<DOCTYPE CORBA [
<!ELEMENT API (#PCDATA)>
<!ELEMENT ORB (#PCDATA)>
<!ELEMENT domain (#PCDATA)
<!ELEMENT service (#PCDATA)
<!ELEMENT facility (PCDATA)
]
```

What does this DTD for you? It gives the basic components or elements of CORBA. Later chapters give the details so that each element of the DTD can become a document type. One could also develop this DTD into a very complex one using attributes with the elements and then making further refinements. The key guideline here is that one can structure an XML DTD for CORBA based on one's skills or needs. There is no one way to do this; you have to decide what the specific design goal is and structure the DTD accordingly.

Note: With HTML one can easily see—because of a logical definition of numbers (not common sense) that 1 goes before 2 in a sequence—that the <h1> tag comes before the <h2> tag, but with XML you have to know what you want to be first and then second. In the DTD example, the order establishes a type of relationship among the five elements, <!ELEMENT ...>.

Chapter 8

Essentials of CORBAservices

Included in This Chapter:

- ❑ CORBAservices Highlights
- ❑ Core Design Principles for CORBAservices
- ❑ Concurrency Control Service Essentials
- ❑ Event Service Essentials
- ❑ Externalization Service Essentials
- ❑ Licensing Service Essentials
- ❑ Life Cycle Service Essentials
- ❑ Naming Service Essentials
- ❑ Object Collections Service Essentials
- ❑ Object Trader Service Essentials
- ❑ Persistent Object Service Essentials
- ❑ Property Service Essentials
- ❑ Query Service Essentials
- ❑ Relationship Service Essentials
- ❑ Security Service Essentials
- ❑ Time Service Essentials
- ❑ Transaction Service Essentials

This chapter briefly looks at CORBAservices to establish descriptive information for the development of a document type definition (DTD) using CORBAservices as a document type labeled *services* (Chapter 12). The information on the services is kept to essentials for DTD design purposes. A Security Service DTD is developed in Chapter 13 with a document type labeled security, and more details are given there.

CORBAservices Highlights

CORBAservices are interfaces that have been standardized by the OMG for use by developers. The manner of implementation is not defined in the model, but the types of interfaces are. Here are the services used to design the CORBAservices DTD in Chapter 12 along with their primary purposes:

CORBAservices	Primary Purposes
Concurrency Control	Regulates resources using a lock manager. Defines locks according to different access categories.
Event	Allows for asynchronous events, event "fan-in," event "fan-out," and reliable event delivery.
Externalization	Provides a standard way for getting data into and out of a component by defining externalization protocols and conventions.
Licensing	Provides a method for metering usage of a component (controls use of intellectual property). Three controls are supported: consumer (user or machine assignment), time (end and start date, duration), and value mapping (for example, resource usage).
Life Cycle	Defines conventions for object creating, deleting, copying, and moving in different locations.
Naming	Enables the location of an object by name (human readable) on the network rather than by address. A key notion is the *naming context* (a set of unique names).
Object Collections	Provides a uniform method to create and manipulate generically the most common collections (groups of objects).
Object Trader	Provides a matchmaking service for objects.
Persistent Object	Allows for an object to be retrieved when there is a system crash.

CORBAservices	Primary Purposes
Property	Permits an object to store information on another object. An application can define a set of standard properties for its objects. These properties could then be handled in a uniform method.
Query	Enables the location of an object to be found by a method other than name such as indexing.
Relationship	Provides a method to create dynamic associations such as one-to-one or one-to-many.
Security	Supports access control, administration, auditing, authentication, authorization, confidentiality, identification, non-repudiation, and secure communications.
Time	Permits synchronization in a distributed environment (current time together with its associated error estimate).
Transaction	Enables an operation to be defined across multiple objects as a single transaction in either a flat or nested model.

Core Design Principles for CORBAservices

This section looks at only a few of the design principles that might be considered relevant to the design of a DTD for the CORBAservices. More technical details are found in the CORBAservices Specification.

A service can be broken up (decomposed) into different interfaces that provide client views. For example, the Event Service has three interfaces: *PushConsumer*, *PullSupplier*, and *Event Channel*.

Some services have callback interfaces. They are required for client objects that support invocation of some operation.

Some services employ element identifiers. The scope of an identifier is limited to a context.

There are two types of return codes—exceptional and normal. The first is represented by error returns, while the second is represented by a DONE return code.

A part of the designing vision is to consider future CORBAservices as their related current services. Here is a list of these services with their associates:

Future Object Services	Associated Services
Archive	Externalization, Persistent Object
Backup/Restore	Externalization, Persistent Object, Transaction
Change Management	Persistent Object
Data Interchange	Externalization, Persistent Object
Implementation Repository	Persistent Object
Internationalization	Naming
Logging	Transaction
Recovery	Transaction
Replication	Persistent Object
Startup	Persistent Object

While CORBAServices do not depend upon specific software, some services have dependencies on other services. Here is a list of the services and whether there are dependencies or not:

Services	Service Needed
Concurrency Control	None
Event	None
Externalization	Life Cycle, Relationship
Licensing	Event, Property, Query, Relationship, Security
Life Cycle	Naming, Relationship
Naming	None
Object Collections	None
Object Trader	None
Persistent Object	Externalization, Life Cycle
Property	None
Query	None
Relationship	None
Security	None
Time	None
Transaction	Concurrency Control, Persistent Object

These design principles can be used in defining attributes and relationships in the DTD.

Some of the attributes may be defined as "yes" or "no."

Concurrency Control Service Essentials

Concurrency Control Service regulates resources using lock management. Locks are defined according to different access categories. This service may be used to restrict the number of clients using a database (only one at a time) or the ability of a client to manipulate a file, either read or write.

The service provides for lock granularity and locking modes. The granularity can be either coarse-grained or fine-grained. There are at least five types of locking modes:

■ Read
■ Write
■ Upgrade
■ Intention Read
■ Intention Write

Note: Perhaps a better name for the Concurrency Control Service is Lock Management Service.

Event Service Essentials

Event Service allows four types of events: asynchronous, "fan-in," "fan-out," and reliable event delivery. The data can be either generic or specific. The three key components of the Event Service architecture are supplier (event data producer), event channel, and consumer (event data processor).

The service uses two models, *push* and *pull*. There can be a push or pull consumer as well as a push or pull supplier. An event channel functionally is all four types.

Event communication can be generic or typed. OMG IDL can describe event communication. There can be proxies for each of the four push/pull and consumer/supplier variations.

Externalization Service Essentials

Externalization Service standardizes a method for getting data into and out of a component by using a set of protocols and conventions. From a programming view an object is externalized at one location and internalized at a remote location. The Externalization Service uses the Relationship Service and the Life Cycle Service to achieve its goals.

Note: The name of this service implies only half of its functions since it also does internalization.

Licensing Service Essentials

Licensing Service provides a method for controlling intellectual property. It uses three types of controls: consumer, time, and value mapping. The interface is generic so a variety of licensing models can be handled such as charge-per-use or charge-per-hour.

These three controls also have attributes:

- Consumer   Assignment and Reservation
- Time   Duration and Expiration
- Value mapping   Allocative, Consumptive, and Unit

Life Cycle Service Essentials

Life Cycle Service is a set of standards for deleting, copying, and moving an object. The implementing programmer must state how the action is to happen. These operations can be performed in different locations.

A key concept of this service is *factory*. Any object that creates other objects is a factory. For example, a factory object would be useful when reports had to be created using compound documents. A factory object might be registered with the Naming Service and Trading Service so other clients can access it.

Naming Service Essentials

Naming Service is the <u>initial</u> service called as soon as a client connects to an ORB. It enables an object to be located by name rather than by address. Two important concepts associated with this service are *naming context* and *naming library*.

The Naming Service handles name associations or name hierarchies. It does not handle such things as what the object does.

Names can be either public or private. A standards body could define a set of objects for public use. Private names could define a set that belongs to a corporation or even an individual.

This service can handle either names for objects or operations. This makes the management of something that is complex a little easier.

A naming context may have an *identifier* field (name of a server), a *kind* field (represents application information), name components, and an unnamed root context. The name components also can have identifier and kind fields.

The organization for naming contexts can be hierarchical or random. This is also true for name components.

A Name needs at least three things. They are:

■ An ORB pointer

■ A server object pointer

■ An unbound sequence that is a path for each naming context that leads to a final name component

Object Collections Service Essentials

Object Collections Service enables a group of objects to be manipulated as one. It handles generically the most common components.

Object Collections Service has a number of interfaces based on collection properties. Here is an abbreviated list of collection properties used:

■ Unordered
  ❏ Unique
    ● Map
    ● KeySet
    ● Set
  ❏ Multiple
    ● Relation
    ● KeyBag
    ● Bag
    ● Heap
■ Ordered
  ❏ Sorted

- Unique
  - ○ SortedMap
  - ○ KeySortedSet
  - ○ SortedSet
- Multiple
  - ○ SortedRelation
  - ○ KeySortedBag
  - ○ SortedBag
❑ Sequential
- Multiple
  - ○ Equality Sequence
  - ○ Sequence

The Collection interface represents the most abstract view of a collection. The interface defines operations for:

■ Adding elements

■ Removing elements

■ Replacing elements

■ Retrieving elements

■ Inquiring collection information

■ Creating iterators

Object Trader Service Essentials

Object Trader Service provides a matchmaking service for objects. It allows an object to publicize and bid for a job. This service is like the telephone Yellow Pages in that it lets you search by category. The Object Trader Service queries five types of offers:

■ Potential

■ Considered

■ Matched

■ Ordered

■ Returned

Persistent Object Service Essentials

Persistent Object Service (POS) allows for an object to be retrieved when there is a system crash. This means an object's state has to be preserved over a period of time. For example, the application that is used to write this document retains the original state of the document when it is revised; the original is hidden from view until such time as the function "save as" is done. This is a simple example of a more complex reality.

Without getting into details, there are certain things one should know about the POS for designing a CORBAservices DTD, such as the basic architectural components and control types.

The fundamental architectural components of the POS may be:

- Client
- Persistent Object and its associated Persistent Identifier
- Persistent Object Manager
- Persistent Data Service and its protocol interface
- Database or a flat file (data storage type)

The two methods for controlling persistence are *connection* and *store/restore*. The two types of connection operations are "connect" and "disconnect." The types of store/restore operations are obvious.

Property Service Essentials

Property Service permits an object to store information on another object. An application can define a set of standard properties (attributes) for its objects so these properties can be handled uniformly. In CORBA parlance an *attribute* is a variable defined in an object's IDL (Interface Definition Language). A *property* has both a name and a value.

Property Service supports a number of operations. The PropertySet interface supports defining, deleting, enumerating, and checking for the existence of properties.

Clients can manipulate property modes individually or in batches. Five mutually exclusive property modes have been defined and they are as follows:

- Normal
- Readonly

- Fixed_Normal
- Fixed_Readonly
- Undefined

Query Service Essentials

Query Service enables an object's location to be found by something other than name, such as indexing. The Query Service specifies an interface so CORBA objects and both object-oriented and relational databases can be viewed as a single query target. A query can be directed toward a single object or a collection of objects.

Query supports interoperability across a variety of query systems by supporting two major query languages. These languages are SQL-92 Query and OQL-93.

Query Service supports major query operations. These operations are selection, insertion, updating, and deletion of collections.

Query Service supports two types of service, Collections and Query Framework. The Collection interface uses association for query, while the Query Framework interface uses association and inheritance.

Query Service defines only a top-level, basic Collection interface that supports query on arbitrary collections without restriction on any particular type. Some of the types commonly used are Equality Collection, Key Collection, and Ordered Collection (Sequential and Sorted).

Relationship Service Essentials

Relationship Service provides a method to create dynamic associations such as one-to-one or one-to-many. All the chapters in this book have been written. It now is time to put them all together; they need to be related. This where the Relationship Service comes to the front. The chapters (files) are distinct objects and need to be related to each other and as a whole. That which is simply stated is not simply done. This is outside of the goals of this book.

The comprehension of the Relationship Service might on first glance appear to be easy; however, that might need a second consideration. Here are five categories of relationships:

Cardinality	Number (maximum) of relationships involved such as a chapter in a book might be related to a number of chapters.
Degree	Number of required roles such as a chapter is a part of a book, a chapter is before and after other chapters, and other chapters reference a chapter.
Roles	Types of relationships an object may assume such as a chapter in the body of the book or an appendix of the book.
Semantics	Defines relationship attributes such as chapter number as the attribute of chapter-order relationship.
Types	Name of the relationships among or between objects such as table of content relationship of chapters to book or the author relationship of a person (writer) to a book.

Security Service Essentials

Security Service supports the basic components of a security policy: access control, administration, auditing, authentication, authorization, confidentiality, identification, non-repudiation, and secure communications. The design for this service is based on a white paper written by security specialists in 1994. This service is discussed in detail in Chapter 13.

Time Service Essentials

Time Service permits synchronization in a distributed environment. It gives the current time together with its associated error parameter. Greenwich Mean Time is the base standard time (referred to in the Specification as Universal Time Coordinate (UTC)), while the base date is October 15, 1582.

Note: When Pope Gregory XIII proclaimed the Gregorian calendar to be the calendar of the Church it was October 15, 1582 (Gregorian calendar), while the prior day was October 4, 1582 (Julian calendar). The Gregorian calendar did not become the dating standard in Europe until the time of the Communist Revolution.

Time Service handles both objects and events. There are two core interfaces, *TimeService* and *TimeEventService*.

Transaction Service Essentials

Transaction Service enables an operation to be defined across multiple objects as a single transaction in either a flat (required) or nested (optional) model. An object is considered either transactional or recoverable. There are four key transaction concepts:

Atomicity	Changes are completely committed (done) or undone.
Consistency	Changes are handled in the same method all the time.
Isolation	Changes are handled independently of each other.
Durability	Changes are persistent.

Transaction Service manages context in two ways, direct and indirect. It handles propagation in two ways, explicit and implicit. The end result is that transactions can be handled in four ways:

■ Direct context with explicit propagation
■ Direct context with implicit propagation
■ Indirect context with explicit propagation
■ Indirect context with implicit propagation

Transaction Service supports application through five basic entities. These entities are:

■ Transactional Client
■ Transactional Objects
■ Recoverable Objects
■ Transactional Servers
■ Recoverable Servers

Transaction Service has a number of interfaces. These interfaces include:

- Coordinator
- Current
- Recovery Coordinator
- Resource
- Subtransaction Aware Resource
- Synchronization
- Terminator
- Transactional Object
- TransactionFactory

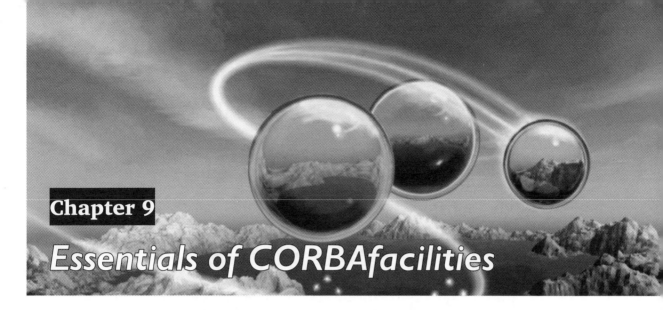

Chapter 9

Essentials of CORBAfacilities

CORBAfacilities is the place in CORBA that is for the end user. This is the place where an end user's formatted document or spreadsheet is handled. This is the area for application development for both horizontal and vertical facilities. A horizontal facility is for the use of almost everyone, such as compound document administration or network (system) administration. A vertical facility is for a specialized market that has many different applications but a common goal (environment), such as publishing or telecommunications.

Note: This is the place of speculation and thoughts on the field of dreams. Using a well-worn cliché, this is an area of dynamic growth.

Perhaps the Object Management Architecture (OMA) can be stated as a simple formula:

ORB = Common Access

CORBAservices = Services for objects

CORBAfacilities = Services for applications

OMA = ORB + CORBAservices + CORBAfacilities

Note: There is more to the OMA than stated above; however, it does cover the basics.

Horizontal common facilities have been broken down into four types. The types are:

■ User Interface (Chapter 2 of the CORBAfacilities Specification)

■ Information Management (Chapter 3 of the CORBAfacilities Specification)

■ Systems Management (Chapter 4 of the CORBAfacilities Specification)

■ Task Management (Chapter 5 of the CORBAfacilities Specification)

Vertical market facilities have been broken down into specialized markets (Chapter 6 of the CORBAfacilities Specification). The markets are:

■ Imagery

■ Information Superhighways

■ Manufacturing

■ Distributed Simulation

■ Oil and Gas Industry

■ Accounting

■ Application Development

■ Mapping

Finally, the place of two CORBAservices, Internationalization and Security, have to be discussed. It is the goal of the OMG that these two CORBAservices support all of the Common Facilities. The language and protection requirements need to be considered for all users.

Note: As with the discussion on CORBAservices in Chapter 8, the goal of this chapter is to look at the architecture rather than the "how-to" for the purpose of gaining information for designing an XML document type definition (DTD) for CORBAfacilities in Chapter 14.

User Interface Facility Essentials

User Interface handles both user access and their needs. The User Interface facility is an interaction between a user and applications. The key components are:

- User interface style
- Workstation hardware
- User interface enablers
  - ❏ Work management system
  - ❏ Task and process automation

To do this the User Interface has been divided into five components:

- Rendering Management
- Compound Presentation
- User Support
- Desktop Management
- Scripting

Rendering and Scripting have general user interfaces, while the other three have special user interfaces for particular domains. Again what is given here on these five components is what is stated publicly rather than what is future development. The key to XML DTD design is to have scalability and flexibility. It is always easier to design the framework than develop the end product.

The Rendering Management Facility provides for output devices such as screens and printers, and for input devices such as a mouse or a keyboard. It includes support for:

- Window management
- Class libraries for user interface objects
- User interface dialogue objects
- Input and output device abstractions

The Compound Presentation Facility provides manipulating functions for window display. Some of the areas to be addressed are:

- Geometry management
- Human interface event distribution
- Shared human interface control management
- Rendering management

The User Support Facility covers cross-application functions such as help and spell and grammar checking. Some of the areas to be addressed are:

- Annotating
- Graphic functions
- Spreadsheet functions
- Versioning

The Desktop Management Facility is ultimately concerned with the end-user's desktop. The facility is to look at three key user objects:

- Information
  - ❑ Aggregations (hierarchies)
  - ❑ Versions (evolution)
  - ❑ Configurations (consistency)
- Tools
  - ❑ Browsers
  - ❑ Editors
  - ❑ System tools (management)
  - ❑ Hardware tools (printers)
- Tasks (based on operational workflow)

The Scripting Facility handles the automation of scripts and functional decomposition. Scripting considers such things as recordings for keystrokes and mouse clicks.

Information Management Facility Essentials

This facility is another one where one can hang out the "Under Construction" sign. The subject subdivisions as compared to operational relationships for this facility are:

- Information modeling
  - ❏ Information storage and retrieval
  - ❏ Information interchange
- Data encoding and representation

From this paradigm six components were defined as key to this facility. Information Management should cover:

- Modeling
- Definition
- Storage
- Retrieval
- Management
- Information Interchange

An Information Modeling Facility's goals are the structuring, accessing, and maintaining of information (data). It should reflect informational models such as relational and object. The facility should describe at least:

- Object interfaces
- Service interfaces
- Object relationships
- Atomic data types

An Information Storage and Retrieval Facility should embrace all database products. This includes text, images, graphics, etc. This facility should be used with a number of domains including:

- Application development
- Data warehousing
- Systems management

A basic issue of retrieval is how to handle metadata. This facility should have interfaces that handle the basic services of an information retrieval system:

- Initialization
- Search
- Retrieve
- Access control
- Termination

Information interchange facilities (Compound Interchange, Data Interchange, and Information Exchange) should allow for exchange of information between users and different software components. This requires conversions among different models, media, and encodings. Basically, this facility handles data interchange in compound documents.

The Compound Interchange Facility should be a framework for data object storage and interchange. It should address data object:

■ Binding

■ Annotation

■ Conversion

■ Exchange

■ Linking

■ Reference storage

The Data Interchange Facility enables objects to be interoperable through data exchanges. This facility allows different forms and kinds of data transfer such as:

■ Domain-specific object representations

■ Formatted data

■ Bulk data transfer

■ Structured data

■ Legacy data

The Information Exchange Facility should enable data exchanges among applications over three layers of interchange. These layers from lowest to highest are:

■ Infrastructure

■ Enabling technology

■ Semantics

This facility needs to handle mediated information exchange. To achieve this goal, four services have to be deployed:

■ Content language

■ Vocabulary

■ Communication

■ Interaction control

Interfaces for a Data Encoding and Representation Facility should support practical interworking and information interchange. The transport modes should include shared storage media, networking protocols, and direct programming interfaces.

The interfaces should specify data types to be encoded and quality of service requirements. There should be at least four interfaces to generalized services for:

■ Data compression

■ Data decompression

■ Representation to canonical conversion

■ Canonical to representation conversion

The Time Operations Facility's purpose is to have interfaces for the manipulation of time and calendar data. There should be capabilities to have services for:

■ Time stamping

■ Time duration

■ Time range

■ Time comparison

■ Time instance manipulation

System Management Facility Essentials

The System Management Facility is concerned with complex, multi-vendor information systems. It should have a set of utility interfaces for system administration functions. Four classes of users have been identified that could be affected by this facility:

■ Users (system administrators)

■ Developers (management application)

■ Service providers (system)

■ Enterprise (resource planners)

As a start, ten System Management Facilities have been identified. They are as follows:

■ Policy Management
  ❏ Policy application for manageable components
  ❏ Manipulation of manageable components

- Quality of Service Management
  - ❑ Availability
  - ❑ Performance
  - ❑ Reliability
  - ❑ Recovery
- Instrumentation
  - ❑ Workload (object creation and deletion counts, etc.)
  - ❑ Object allocation to physical resources
  - ❑ Responsiveness
- Data Collection
  - ❑ Logging
  - ❑ History Management
- Security Management
- Collection Management
  - ❑ Queried
  - ❑ Applied
- Instance Management
- Scheduling Management
- Customization
- Event Management
  - ❑ Generation
  - ❑ Registration
  - ❑ Filtration
  - ❑ Aggregation
  - ❑ Event notification

Task Management Facility Essentials

Task Management Facility's goals are to handle the automation of user and system processes. The facility should be a set of interfaces for the task management infrastructure. Four facilities are considered as points of development:

- Workflow
  - ❑ Flows
  - ❑ Long transactions

- Agent
  - ❏ Functions
    - ● Agent off-load
    - ● Load bookkeeping
  - ❏ Agent
    - ● Mobile
      - ○ Control Service
      - ○ Communication Service
      - ○ Message Service
    - ● Static
      - ○ Basic Information Services
      - ○ Simple Query Services
      - ○ Multi-response Services
      - ○ Assertion Services
      - ○ Generation Services
      - ○ Capability Services
      - ○ Notification Services
      - ○ Extension Services
        - ➤ Networking Services
        - ➤ Facilitation Services
        - ➤ Database Services
        - ➤ Adaptation Services
        - ➤ Error Correction Services
        - ➤ Automatic Retransmission Services
        - ➤ Registration Service
          - ➢ Home
          - ➢ Visitor
        - ➤ Security Services
          - ➢ Response encryption
          - ➢ Access control
        - ➤ Management Services
- Rule Management
  - ❏ Scripting
  - ❏ Storage
  - ❏ Interpretation

■ Automation
  ❑ Method Invocation
  ❑ Object Specifier

Vertical Facilities Essentials

Vertical facilities define unique requirements within a specific market. This area has great potential for growth, particularly by standards groups and industrial alliances. Some of the market facilities that have been defined are as follows:

■ Imagery
■ Information Superhighways
■ Manufacturing
■ Distributed Simulation
■ Oil and Gas Industry
■ Accounting
■ Application Development
■ Mapping

The Imagery Facility should be able to have interfaces that handle imagery interchange, *imagery* being a two- or more dimensional data array derived either from sensors or produced artificially. The facility should include imagery manipulations for:

■ Examining
■ Processing
■ Annotating
■ Storing
■ Displaying

The Information Superhighways Facility could be called the Intranet/ Internet Facility because of its associated protocols and conventions. The basic infrastructure of this facility is:

■ Commercial Operations Facility
  ❑ Advertisement
  ❑ Monitoring
  ❑ Costing
■ Resource Discovery Facility

- ■ Intermediaries Facility
  - ❏ Broker
  - ❏ Intelligent agent
  - ❏ Mediator
  - ❏ Trader
- ■ Teleconferencing Facilities
  - ❏ Collaboration
  - ❏ Mentoring
- ■ Experimentation Facility
- ■ User Access Facility
  - ❏ Interface level (novice or expert)
  - ❏ User profile management
  - ❏ Group association

The Manufacturing Facility represents integration of computational and manufacturing resources. Three areas have been identified for development:

- ■ Policy variable management (business rules)
- ■ History management
  - ❏ Access
  - ❏ Control
- ■ Product data service (STEP standards)
  - ❏ Concurrent engineering support
  - ❏ Information technological integration support
  - ❏ Encapsulated object-oriented interface
  - ❏ Fast execution of large models of fine-grained objects

The Distributed Simulation Facility should have facilities for simulations for air traffic control, war gaming, and video games. This facility should have at least these services:

- ■ Simulation management
  - ❏ Simulation configuring
  - ❏ Component choosing
  - ❏ Connection specifying
  - ❏ Component allocating
  - ❏ Component instantiating
  - ❏ Component start ensuring

- ❏ Component status monitoring
- ❏ Component shut-down
- ❏ Simulation identifying
- ❏ Component state checking
■ Time management
- ❏ Initial simulation time prior to start
- ❏ Basic component commands (start, pause, resume, and stop)
■ Aircraft and vehicle state
- ❏ Entity maintenance and administration
- ❏ Database snapshots
- ❏ Callback establishments
- ❏ State information
■ Flight data
- ❏ Allows components to subscribe or unsubscribe
- ❏ Publishes initial plans and changes to subscribers
■ Adaptation
- ❏ Location of airways
- ❏ Fixes
- ❏ Airspace definitions
■ Environment
- ❏ Weather
- ❏ Terrain

The Oil and Gas Industry Exploration and Production Facility is concerned with process. The business processes involve a large quantity of data, complex algorithms, and long-term data storage.

The Accounting Facility is concerned with the computer type as compared to the manual type. The facility seeks to resolve the business reality that most accounting software interfaces are custom-designed and proprietary. The facility should involve:

■ Money exchange
■ Payroll
■ Purchases
■ Sales
■ Online charges

The Application Development Facility covers the selection, development, building, and evolution of enterprise information systems. The referenced model is for describing the environments that support projects that engineer, develop, and manage computer-based systems (object-oriented). Basic expected interfaces are as follows:

■ Technical engineering
  ❏ System
  ❏ Software
  ❏ Process
■ Applications components for reuse
  ❏ Frameworks and patterns
  ❏ Domain-specific
■ Technical management
  ❏ Change
  ❏ Reuse
■ Project management
  ❏ Plan
  ❏ Estimate
  ❏ Risk analysis
  ❏ Tracking
■ Support
  ❏ Text processing
  ❏ Numeric processing
  ❏ Figure processing
■ Framework
  ❏ Object management
  ❏ Process management
  ❏ Communication
  ❏ Operating system
  ❏ User
  ❏ Policy enforcement

The Mapping Facility covers those services required for applications that access and display geospatial data. A function not to be covered is analysis; however, the two that are to be covered are:

■ Access
■ Display

Three basic requirements have been identified for this facility. They are as follows:

■ Database querying
■ Access to modeling and analysis facilities
■ Presentation production assistance

Essentials on CORBAservices Support

It is the goal of the OMG that two CORBAservices, Internationalization and Security, support all of the Common Facilities. The language and protection requirements need to be considered for all users.

Internationalization means that users can work with and in their own language and cultural conventions. The Internationalization Facility allows:

■ Language support for operating system
■ Language for stored information
■ User's mathematical conventions
■ User's date and time conventions
■ User's currency conventions
■ User's text sorting and string comparing conventions
■ User's rendering for page display conventions

The Security Facility is concerned with the management of the variety of OMA-compliant security systems. The facility is to be designed and developed using the *OMG White Paper on Security* (1994). The goal is to have a set of interfaces that do not affect the core security of a system.

Part III

XML Applications

Included in This Part:

- Chapter 10—Design and Development Issues

- Chapter 11—Designing an XML DTD for CORBA Domains

- Chapter 12—Designing an XML DTD for CORBAservices

- Chapter 13—Designing an XML DTD for the Security Service

- Chapter 14—Designing an XML DTD for CORBAfacilities

- Chapter 15—Final Thoughts, Summary, and Conclusions

Chapter 10
Design and Development Issues

Whether one is deigning to use CORBA, XML, Java, or HTML, there are some basic software design principles that should be adhered to at all times. Here are ten design and development principles:

■ Abstraction

■ Flexibility

■ Interoperability

■ Modularity

■ Reconfigurability

■ Reusability

■ Scalability

■ Simplicity

Part III

■ Stability

■ Use good project management practices

Above the door or on the wall of any design group should be written, "Know Thy Subject." This means one does not sit down and start programming or doing XML markup when one gets a project. This chapter discusses some design issues for CORBA and some for XML.

Besides the preceding list of general principles, one needs to consider specific issues. These issues come in two categories, single environment or multiple environments. This chapter discusses both categories for CORBA, XML, HTML, and Java.

In some cases, "it is" statements are given. One might immediately wonder why that statement is an issue. The reply is that if you do not think about the obvious, it can become an issue. For example, CORBA is fundamentally a set of standard interfaces concerned with services of various aggregations: single service, a group of services (facilities), and groups of services (domains). What does this mean to you as a developer? No matter what programming or markup language you use, your implementation involves interface design issues.

General Software Design and Development Principles

There are nine software design principles given and one fundamental project management principle. The last one has its own set of guidelines. Some basic project management guidelines are given with a minimal of clarification. The nine software design principles could be stated in a number of ways.

Abstraction

Why should a programmer be concerned with abstraction? One has to be concerned about CORBA objects, an abstraction. A network infrastructure is made of concrete and abstract components. A concrete component would be a computer, while the abstract component is the scalability of the computer or the amount of upgrade possible. Another abstract example that is very pertinent to software design is life cycle.

Flexibility

Flexibility does not mean instability. It means having system modules that can handle change. For example, domain properties are probably unknown as of the beginning of the development. One should design a module to handle these properties as development progresses.

Interoperability

Interoperability means literally "between operations," or to what degree one operation works with another. The operations can be either features (functionality) or data interchange. Some of the problems of interoperability are handled by CORBA. CORBA has the Object Service definitions that are uniform access mechanisms that handle universal communications. In XML you have to consider elements as parsed or unparsed data.

Modularity

Modularity is the ability to design a system that separates components (modules) to handle stability and flexibility issues. For CORBA, the use of the Interface Definition Language (IDL) results in a hierarchy of files such as base class interfaces and APIs.

Reconfigurability

When one considers reconfigurability, one has to consider metadata. Metadata describes data (attributes and formats). It is the resource that eliminates hard coding all calls to a service. Reconfigurability or symmetry is writing common interfaces. Each interface can be implemented for a broad area of services, facilities, or applications.

Reusability

Reusability means that the code or markup can be used for more than one function or data type. A key principal object-oriented method for code reusability is inheritance. CORBA supports inheritance at the interface level. An important tool for assisting in the code reusability design is the Interface Definition Language (IDL).

Scalability

Scalability, or extensibility, is the ability for the system to grow or adapt. This principle is basic to software life cycle architecture. Scalability is not functionality (number of features). It is the opportunity for increased functionality. One needs to consider compatibility of code design and data format.

Simplicity

Simplicity is probably the most important design principle. Is the code or markup easy to read? Have the customer's stated goals been done, neither less nor more? The key phrase is "nor more." There is a tendency to enhance the code. To program something because it is a nice idea is not simplicity; it is duplicity. Do not confuse simplicity with functionality. Functionality means a new feature is added. Has the functionality been stated in the written goals agreed upon by the customer?

Stability

A complete system (complex program implementation) cannot be designed as stable, but some parts can be considered stable. These parts or system modules should be designed as "separate" components. A critical system component is the API designs.

Use Good Project Management Practices

What is given here is a nutshell, a very small one at that, on correct basic project management guidelines. You may state a solution in a brief paragraph when you do a very simple design program or you may need reams of paper for a complex project. The guidelines given here are for an XML project. For CORBA, guidelines 1-5 and 10 are pertinent.

Guideline 1: Define Goals and Customer Expectations

Because XML permits you to define your own tag sets (start-tag and end-tags as well as the content type that is delimited by these two tags) or an empty-element tag, one needs to establish clearly one's design goals. Also, XML is used to handle both text and data transactions.

Guideline 2: Define Control Process

There is the tendency to define the quality control process, if at all, at the end of a project definition. Testing criteria should be established up front because these criteria are usually stated in the context of the known. You are seeking to achieve success in an unknown environment.

Guideline 3: Define Skill Process

Defining the skill requirements is different from defining the people requirements. The resource requirements, materials, and equipment are inherent to Guideline 5. It is not the number of people that matters, but the skill levels and types available either internally or externally. A skill level can range from a novice to an expert.

Guideline 4: Define Time Requirements

Only two dates are really important to a project. They are the start date and the customer's expected end date. The ultimate question is "Can the expected goals be achieved realistically by the end date?" If not, negotiate a new end date if possible. All other dates are just management milestones to achieve success.

Guideline 5: Define Resource Requirements

This guideline is concerned with the materials and equipment requirements. In a small design and development project, the materials and equipment required are probably easily or already available. The materials and equipment may not be available for a large project.

Guideline 6: Design an XML Document

Designing an XML document follows the basic ideas of good programming. Basically outline what you want to do, develop testing criteria, develop what you said you would do, test what you said you would do by the stated testing criteria, and implement what you said you have done in a production environment. The devil is in the details.

Guideline 7: Develop an XML Document

One needs to create a goal definition and a core document type definition (DTD) before developing the markup for the XML. The key to developing an XML is to have:

■ A goal definition

- A document type definition (DTD) based on the goal definition
- Markup based on the DTD
- Adherence (conformance) to the well-formedness and validity constraints

Guideline 8: Adhere to Well-Formedness Constraints

The rule for violating a well-formedness constraint is harsh, in fact, it is fatal. Any validating processor must report this type of violation in the content of the document entity (the root entity where the processor starts validation) and any other parsed entity and stop its processing.

Guideline 9: Adhere to Validity Constraints

Not adhering to a validity constraint may or may not cause an error. However, a valid XML document adheres to all these constraints. A validating XML processor must report errors of validity constraints at the user's option. User's option means you can enable or disable the reporting mechanism for these constraints.

Guideline 10: Consider Special Local Situation

There is no one answer for every situation and every location. You do need to consider your environment. You must factor in legacy. Legacy is any software you have placed in production status or any hardware now active in the system.

Some CORBA Design Issues

CORBA is fundamentally a set of standard interfaces concerned with services of various aggregations: single service, a group of services (facilities), and groups of services (domains). What does this mean to you as a developer? No matter what programming or markup language you use, your implementation involves interface design issues.

You need to identify the places of definition and modeling languages in your design process. Chapter 5 covers Distributed Component Architecture Modeling (DCAM), Organization Management Group's (OMG) Interface Definition Language (IDL), and Rational Software's Unified Modeling Language. Chapter 6 covers webMethods' Web Interface Definition Language (WIDL).

You need to select a formal methodology that includes object-oriented analysis. This means you should do some up front planning rather than just sit down and start coding. You can use paper or a computer, just have an organized strategy. Chapter 7 gives a broad sweep of the structure of CORBA. Chapters 8 and 9 detail the architecture of CORBAservices and CORBAfacilites for designing XML document type definitions in Chapters 11 through 14.

The first level of design should pertain to states of objects (local variables). This part of the design plan should state which variables are IDL attributes.

Since you are working with CORBA you are implementing an application in a distributed system. Object selection should use this fact as a criterion in identifying applicable objects.

When you name your objects, consider how these names might be used with IDL. IDL does require consistency in naming conventions because some of the language binding is case-dependent.

For an ORB product to be compliant it must comply with the CORBA Core Specification and have an IDL compiler for at least one programming language. What must be adhered to are the:

- CORBA Object Model
- CORBA architecture
- OMG IDL syntax and semantics
- Dynamic Invocation Interface (DII)
- Dynamic Skeleton Interface (DSI)
- Interface Repository (IR)
- ORB Interface
- Basic Object Adapter

Note: This book is concerned with the CORBA model and architecture for designing XML document type definitions that reflect the implications of CORBA general design principles.

Your user role has an impact on your design. The magic word is *interoperability*. In a distributed system you can have one or more of these roles:

- User
- Administrator or maintainer
- Object developer
- ORB agent (one who implements)

Each of the roles requires a different level of comprehension and perspective of CORBA. The user views CORBA in a transparent manner while the developer must know all the nuts and bolts. A developer does not just know some of the rules but all the rules, and adheres to them.

For CORBA designing one needs to comprehend the boundaries of domains, services, facilities, and APIs. In comparison one needs to know the implications of XML logical and physical structures and the resulting elements, attributes, and entities.

If one uses Rational Software Corporation's Unified Modeling Language (UML) as a part of one's design methodology, one must consider a key element of UML, the *class diagram*. A class diagram describes classes and their static relationships to other classes. From a class diagram, one might select classes that might be used to declare XML elements and entities. Can a relationship be considered an XML attribute?

Perhaps a design principle can be established for relating IDL and XML. IDL is a definition language that defines interfaces in CORBA. XML is a markup language that can declare the structures of CORBA interfaces using the document metaphor.

Note: The word used with XML is "declare" rather than "define" since you have element, attribute, and entity declarations.

Some XML DTD Design Issues

To use the full functionality of XML one must have a document type definition (DTD). Yes, you can do XML markup without a DTD by using an implied one. A DTD is used to define or declare the rules of your markup. Without your own DTD you must follow or adhere to some else's rules and you may not get what you expect.

Note: You can actually use a set of document type definitions. The XML dialect Chemical Markup Language (CML) uses three. This book discusses four DTDs that might be considered integral to each other.

In the section called "Use Good Project Management Practices" earlier in this chapter, the example guidelines given are pertinent to XML. The ones that should be written and kept where you can see them at all times are:

■ Guideline 1: You define you own tag sets (start-tag and end-tag) or empty-element tag.

■ Guideline 8: Adhere to well-formedness constraints. (Listed in Appendix D)

■ Guideline 9: Adhere to validity constraints. (Listed in Appendix D)

Note: Well-formedness and validity processor constraints are discussed in the context of production rules in Chapter 2. As a part of XML jargon, XML documents are *well-formed* and *valid*.

XML was <u>not</u> designed or developed to replace HTML. XML was designed to enhance a subset of SGML to enable SGML legacy documents to be used on the Internet. XML uses the logical and physical document metaphor. In an object-oriented environment, a document might be used as an object or a class.

XML looks like and feels like HTML; however, it does not taste like it. XML has tag sets and they must be used in pairs, <u>no</u> <u>exception</u>. XML is more concerned with structure than form. XML design has to be based on a set of production rules (89) and a set of processor constraints (31) rather than rules for tags as is in HTML.

The basic rule of system designing is the system requirements and capabilities. This activity should lead to defining system objects. Why is this important? You could have a document type called system (a document description) that has at least these three declared elements. This DTD could initially begin as:

```
<!DOCTYPE system [
<!ELEMENT system          (requirement, capability, object)+ >
<!ELEMENT requirement     (#PCDATA) >
<!ELEMENT capability      (#PCDATA) >
<!ELEMENT object          (#PCDATA) >
]>
```

Note: See Chapter 3 for a further discussion on designing an XML DTD.

Some HTML Design Issues

HTML and XML were developed from the same source, Standard General-ized Markup Language (SGML). This makes them siblings—children of a common source. HTML represents a Web *page* markup language, while XML represents a Web *document* markup language. One gives links; the other gives structure.

HTML has a defined set of tags. In many cases it is easy to understand the ordering or nesting of the tags, such as <h1> before <h2> and that <h1> should not be nested inside <h2>. An XML DTD establishes the ordering and nesting rules for a document type.

HTML permits you on occasion to omit the end-tag while XML does not. Perhaps this capability is more an implementation issue than a design issue. If you want to translate HTML to XML, this becomes a real issue with a complex page document.

If the appearance of an HTML file on the Web is more important than structure, then converting an HTML file to XML may lead to an unsatisfactory conclusion. XML is not a formatting language. One way this problem is being resolved is through the Extensible Stylesheet Language (XSL).

Note: There are a number of efforts going on to resolve differences between HTML and XML. However, this discussion is limited primarily to designing XML document type definitions in the context of CORBA.

Some Java Design Issues

The concern here is with design, not implementation. It is the knowledge of the architecture of CORBA, the structure of an XML DTD, and the prior-ity of HTML tags that can impact Java programming design. It is the equating of CORBA objects, XML elements and HTML tags to Java's classes, interfaces, packages, and tokens.

Any design with Java has to consider the degree of two implementations. The first is found in Java Platform 1.2 API Specification, package org.omg.CORBA. The second is IBM packages for the Java API, org.w3c.dom and com.ibm.xml.parser.

Note: JDK 1.2 provides Java IDL as an Object Request Broker (ORB).

There are a number of efforts going on to resolve the integration of Java as an operating language and XML as a markup language. However, this discussion is limited primarily to designing XML document type definitions in the context of CORBA.

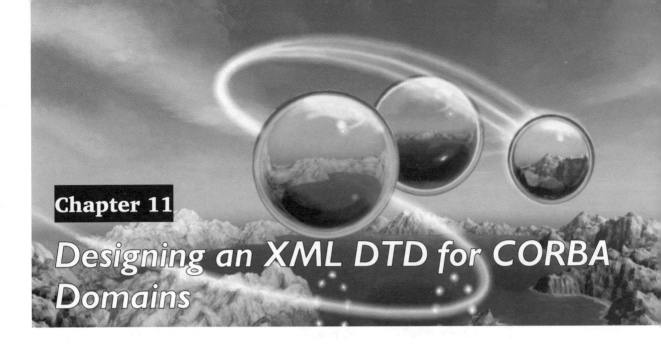

Chapter 11

Designing an XML DTD for CORBA Domains

This chapter considers the design issues for developing XML DTDs for CORBA domains at a very high level. It is important to distinguish among three major parts (CORBAservices, CORBAfacilities, and domains) of the CORBA infrastructure, a structure that is concrete and abstract. While one might see these parts as blocks connected to an Object Request Broker (ORB), one could visualize these parts together without their distinctive relations to the ORB as a pyramid with CORBAservices on the bottom, CORBAfacilities in the middle, and domains on top. Another visual would be a set of circles like a bull's-eye with the inner circle being CORBAservices and the outside one being domains.

Now that you are confused trying to do visuals, let's try three definitions. The key word is service in each definition.

- CORBAservices provide services for objects.
- CORBAfacilities provide services for applications.
- CORBA domains provide services for functions.

One of the many definitions for "service" is "work for another." Another definition is "an act of assistance." Perhaps a contextual definition is that these three CORBA components, sets of interfaces, process variables that are defined by objects, applications, or functions.

Now that the word "service" is as clear as the Mississippi River, what is a "domain"? Perhaps more clearly, what types of domains are being defined by or may be defined by CORBA committees? Some potential types of domains are management, language, security, telecommunications, electronic commerce, financial, and transportation. Some domains may further extend services or facilities such as security or electronic commerce from the facility accounting.

The premise here is that an XML document can handle data and that one can also use the concepts developed for CORBA domains as a starting point for eventual CORBA/XML integration.

The information here is a loosely defined structure for looking at the issue of CORBA/XML integration for domains. A number of actions have to be completed prior to having a clearly defined model. The obvious first step is the development of clear or clearer definitions for basic CORBA- services and CORBAfacilities by the various CORBA development committees.

Also see Chapter 12 (Services) and Chapter 14 (Facilities) for parallel thoughts on this type of activity. This chapter looks at the potential use of CORBA domains and of XML with various domains through discussions of seven interoperability issues.

Declaring the Document Type: Domains

The first two declarations required are an XML declaration (Rule 23) and a document type declaration (Rule 28). Also included at this point is the element type declaration (Rule 39) for domains. Everything else goes between the start of the document type declaration and the end "]>". This document type of *domains* implies that a full set of CORBA domains includes the specified features (interfaces). Also included as appropriate are attributes, entities, and notations. All of these declarations constitute the <u>document type definition</u> (DTD).

```
<?xml version="1.0">
<DOCTYPE domains [
<!ELEMENT domains (reference, … , transaction)>
]<
```

The data that goes within the ellipsis are the other interoperability areas for any CORBA domain. This chapter looks at seven interoperability areas. Included here are brief discussions of DTD design considerations for creating a separate DTD for each interoperability area.

Note: The CORBA Specification V2.2 does refer to the interoperability issues or areas as domains. This discussion tries to consider that any idea given here is evolving. As there are common services, there may be common domains.

Some of the interoperability areas are changed for ease of markup, such as addressing for Network Addressing. The seven areas used in this chapter are as follows:

■ Reference
■ Represent (Representation)
■ Addressing (Network Addressing)
■ Connect (Network Connectivity)
■ Security
■ Type
■ Transaction

Note: Security can be considered a CORBAservice, a CORBAfacility, and a CORBA domain. See Chapters 12, 13, and 14 for further comments on this matter.

Each of the following seven sections are high-level speculations on designing the logical and physical structure of an XML DTD called domains. The number of elements with the DTD are open for discussion. However, there must be at least one entity, the document entity, or as labeled here, domains.

Warning: The information given here should be considered a minimal beginning, perhaps not even a real start. It is a form of speculation (less formulated than ideas) for relating concepts from CORBA with those from XML.

One defines any interoperability area by its scope. A scope establishes a range of operations or a place where there is a common view of interoperability. Why are interoperability areas (issues) used instead of a potential domain such as telecommunications? There are two reasons. The first is the key word "potential." The second is that no matter what domains are developed they have seven issues that must be resolved in the design.

Note: This author was once involved in the issue of writing on-the-job-training (OJT) manuals for a number of managers. I said first write one manual and then change the jargon and the adjective level of authority or responsibility (company, division, or department). The same can be said here also. A domain acts as a type of service manager. Any proper domain design responds to seven interoperability issues within a specialized language. A file in telecommunications for a telephone switch may be called a "table" and in electronic commerce an "account," but in both cases they have to be referenced, represented, addressed, connected to others of the same nature, secured, typed, and have identified types of transactions.

Before Declaring Any Element

Before one can look at declaring an element for the document type domains, one must consider the architecture or model for CORBA domains. This model includes:

■ Technical definition of domain
■ Bridging
■ Place of ORBs
■ Definition of interoperability
■ Architecture of interoperability

These five areas should be used in the fundamental design of the seven components of the domains DTD. For example, one might need to declare bridge types.

The CORBA Specification says that a domain partitions a system into component collections that have a set of common characteristics. A domain's scope is a collection of objects and is a member of the domain through association with common characteristics. In each of the following sections, a scope definition is given for each element. For example, the common characteristic for reference is <u>meaning</u> or the <u>object reference</u> (objref).

One can relate domains in two ways, *containment* and *federation*. First, *containment* is where one domain resides within another. Second, *federation* is where two or more domains are related through a mutual agreement. The mutual administrators set up a federation.

A *bridge* is a mapping mechanism that serves as a kind of "translator" to handle requests between domains. A bridge resides at the boundary between the domains. A bridge more technically stated is an "inter-ORB bridge."

Bridging, the action of the bridge, is to handle an invocation between a client and a server object. Each of course is in a different domain. There are two types of bridging:

■ In-line
■ Request-level

A bridge needs also to manage proxy objects. There are two proxy management techniques:

■ Reference translation
■ Reference encapsulation

Everything seems to come in pairs. There are two types of request-level bridges:

■ Interface-specific
■ Generic

Within the CORBA Core Specifications some interfaces have been defined that are relevant to developing a generic request-level bridge. Five of these interfaces are:

■ CORBA Object References
■ Dynamic Invocation Interface (DII)
■ Dynamic Skeleton Interface (DSI)
■ Interface Repositories
■ Object Adapters

An ORB's place in life is to handle messaging in a transparent manner. A consequence of this transparency is interoperability. Any given CORBA service can be handled separately or independently with one or more domain. Do not expect a universal ORB. Expect vendors to develop meaningful, that means marketable, ORBs.

One can have at least seven interoperability concerns as given above. One can have a broad non-meaningful definition of interoperability or one can have a meaningful one within a specific context such as the structure of CORBA.

One way to look at interoperability is to consider its elements, not XML elements. There are at least three identified elements:

■ ORB interoperability architecture
■ Inter-ORB support
■ General and Internet inter-ORB Protocols (GIOPs and IIOPs)

A second way to look at interoperability is through relationships. The centerpiece is the method of selecting CORBAservices to CORBA domains. The method created may be how one resolves the seven interoperability issues.

The ORB interoperability has two interesting keystones for its framework. The first keystone is having either *immediate* or *mediated* bridging. The second keystone is the implementation of *half-bridges* for mediated bridge domains.

When there need to be local control domains, there is the need for inter-ORB bridge support. This support element specifies ORB APIs and conventions to ensure the appropriate content and semantics mapping controls. This function is not a CORBA responsibility but one for vendors or system administrators.

When one looks at the protocol issues, one needs to think about protocol issues in general as well as CORBA specific. A specific instance is a relationship of protocols and IDL.

Note: The element declarations given here are primarily placeholder because attribute lists have to be agreed upon by two or more domain administrators.

Declaring Element Type: Reference

Reference is the scope of an object reference (objref). It identifies where an object has meaning.

```
<!ELEMENT reference EMPTY >
<!ATTLIST reference meaning CDATA #REQUIRED >
```

This simple example requires a meaningful name for an object reference.

Declaring Element Type: Represent

Representation's scope is the transfer syntax and protocol for a message. It is the location where a message can be received and interpreted.

```
<!ELEMENT represent EMPTY >
<!ATTLIST represent
        syntax CDATA #REQUIRED
        protocol CDATA #REQUIRED >
```

For representation to define a location, one needs stated message syntax and a protocol name.

Declaring Element Type: Addressing

The scope of networking addressing is all the addresses of the network. This is the identification of the location where addresses can be comprehended and retrieved.

```
<!ELEMENT addressing EMPTY >
```

This example is a placeholder.

Declaring Element Type: Connect

The scope of network connectivity is the potential or extent of the paths available for messaging. This element is for declaring the hardware endpoints for the connections of object references and object implementation.

```
<!ELEMENT connect EMPTY >
<ATTLIST  connect
        objref CDATA #REQUIRED
        objimp CDATA #REQUIRED >
```

In this example the two key attributes for connection identification are declared. The attribute contents should be the name of an object reference and its associated object implementation.

Declaring Element Type: Security

The scope is the degree of enforceable security. It is a reflection of a security policy. It is important to design in the context of the security defined for CORBAservices and CORBAfacilities.

```
<!ELEMENT security EMPTY >
```

This is a placeholder. One needs to consider accountability, accessibility, and confidentiality. For further information on security, see Chapter 13.

As a part of the ORB Interoperability Architecture, at least three types of security domains have been defined. They are policy, environment, and technological.

A security policy domain governs aspects as determined by the security authority that needs to be enforced. This is where the security authority's scope is delimited. This is the place for rules and criteria for:

- Access control
- Accountability
- Authentication
- Delegation

Note: Two concerns are the domain's levels of scalability and granularity.

Policy can be impacted by at least four types of domain relationship types. Broadly stated these types are:

- Hierarchy
- Federation
- System
- Application

CORBA has considered two types of environmental domains for security, message protection, and object identity. In either case, these domains should not be visible to applications or Security Services.

The security technological domain is based on the methods of the Authentication services. The technological domain is concerned with the how-to of the policy domain.

Declaring Element Type: Type

The scope of the element is an object's type identifier. This type should be meaningful and known.

```
<!ELEMENT type EMPTY>
```

This is a placeholder.

Declaring Element Type: Transaction

This element identifies the scope of a given transaction service. It is the location allowed for a particular transaction service to be interoperable.

```
<!ELEMENT transaction EMPTY>
```

This is a placeholder.

Possible XML Solution

Recognizing that domain is more encompassing than either CORBAservices or CORBAfacilites for handling a number of services, then perhaps the DTD should be more of a "traffic cop," like the one standing in the middle of the street when a traffic light goes off, for processing applications and external databases.

Some of the design considerations are:

■ Have pointers to files that have the variables required for associated CORBAservices or CORBAfacilities.

■ Have pointers to processing applications.

■ Have controlling variables within the DTD.

Until there is a clearer definition of CORBA domains, one should look at the potential of XML rather than the actual uses of XML in this area.

Note: Microsoft has generated an "evolutionary" stage of XML that may be used in this area. The concept is "data islands." At this time it is not a part of the XML standard.

Chapter 12

Designing an XML DTD for CORBAservices

This chapter uses the premise that an XML document can handle data and that CORBA is fundamentally a series of interfaces; thus, one can design an XML document that organizes and declares the variables that might go into the interfaces. This chapter uses "brainstorming" to state important concepts about the structures and values of CORBAservices interfaces that are necessary knowledge for the fundamentals for planning, designing, and developing any XML DTD or DTDs for CORBAservices. The brainstorming information comes from Chapter 8 and from the CORBAservices Specification (various chapters are dated 1996-1997).

The idea for a document type definition (DTD) for CORBAservices as given here is broadly structured using the interfaces for declaring XML elements. The information given here is a high-level <u>guideline</u> (a way, not <u>the</u> way) for looking at the issue of CORBA/XML integration. It is recognized that an object-oriented programming language such as Java would be required to complete this integration.

In Chapter 13 the Security Service details more than the other services in this chapter. Also see Chapter 11 (Domains) and Chapter 14 (Facilities) for parallel considerations.

Declaring the Document Type: Services

The first two declarations required are an XML declaration (Rule 23) and a document type declaration (Rule 28). Also included at this point is the element type declaration (Rule 39) for services. Everything else goes between the start of the document type declaration and the end "]>". This document of services says that a full set of CORBAservices includes the specified features (interfaces). Also included are appropriate attributes, entities, and notations. All of these declarations constitute the <u>document type definition</u> (DTD).

```
<?xml version="1.0">
<DOCTYPE services [
<!ELEMENT services (naming, … , collections)>
]<
```

The data that goes within the ellipsis are the other 13 services. Five of the service names are changed for ease of markup (Life Cycle, Persistent Object, Concurrency Control, Object Trader, and Object Collections). The 15 services as used in this chapter are as follows:

- Naming
- Event
- Persistent
- LifeCycle
- Concurrency
- Externalization
- Relationship
- Transaction
- Query
- Licensing
- Property
- Time
- Security
- Trader
- Collections

Each of the following sections begins with a kind of brainstorming of each service based on information from Chapter 8 and from the CORBAservices Specification. The focus of the brainstorming is to establish a "draft" framework of the logical structure of each service. This in turn is the basis for developing a logical XML structure and in some cases an enhanced physical structure for a service. There is one necessary entity, the document entity.

Warning: The information given here should <u>NOT</u> be considered complete. It is procedural guidelines for relating concepts from CORBA with those from XML. These declarations are commented to reflect possible alternatives to the ones given.

Declaring Element Type: Naming

Here are some basic points one might get from brainstorming about the Naming Service:

- Initial service called
- Four interfaces
    - LName
    - LNameComponent

- ❏ NamingContext
- ❏ BindingIterator
∎ Key concepts
  - ❏ Name binding
  - ❏ Naming context
  - ❏ Naming Library
∎ Names can be simple or compound (sequence)
∎ Name component has
  - ❏ Name
  - ❏ Identifier attribute
  - ❏ Kind attribute
∎ Handles name associations or hierarchies
∎ Names can be public or private
∎ Name needs
  - ❏ ORB pointer
  - ❏ Server object pointer
  - ❏ Unbound sequence path
∎ Need to know values for each interface

With these brainstorming ideas and technical data from the Specification, one can begin to declare the <!ELEMENT naming>.

```
<- - Naming Service has four interfaces. - ->
<!ELEMENT naming (LName, LNameComponent, NamingContext,
BindingIterator)>
<!ELEMENT LName EMPTY>
<!ATTLIST LName name CDATA #REQUIRED
              id CDATA #REQUIRED
              kind CDATA #REQUIRED>
<!ELEMENT LNameComponent EMPTY>
<!ELEMENT NamingContext EMPTY>
<!ELEMENT BindingIterator EMPTY>
```

The EMPTY content specification type used with the entire "interface elements" permits attribute lists to define values where appropriate.

Declaring Element Type: Event

Here are some basic points one might get from brainstorming about the Event Service:

- Event types
  - ❑ Asynchronous
  - ❑ "Fan-in"
  - ❑ "Fan-out"
  - ❑ Reliable event delivery
- Seven interfaces
  - ❑ PushSupplier
  - ❑ SupplierAdmin
  - ❑ ProxyPushConsumer
  - ❑ EventChannel
  - ❑ PullConsumer
  - ❑ ConsumerAdmin
  - ❑ ProxyPullSupplier
- Key components
  - ❑ Consumer
  - ❑ Supplier
  - ❑ Event channel
- Data either generic or specific
- Uses push and pull models
- Communication either generic or typed
- Proxy types
  - ❑ Push/consumer
  - ❑ Pull/consumer
  - ❑ Push/supplier
  - ❑ Pull/supplier

```
<- - Event Service has seven interfaces. - ->
<!ELEMENT event (PushSupplier, SupplierAdmin, ProxyPushConsumer, Event
            Channel, PullConsumer, ConsumerAdmin, ProxyPullSupplier)>
<!ELEMENT PushSupplier EMPTY>
<!ELEMENT SupplierAdmin EMPTY>
```

```
<!ELEMENT ProxyPushConsumer EMPTY>
<- - Put values in a file called PPCdb.xml - ->
<!ENTITY PPCdb SYSTEM "PPCdb.xml">
<!ELEMENT EventChannel EMPTY>
<!ELEMENT PullConsumer EMPTY>
<!ELEMENT ConsumerAdmin EMPTY>
<!ELEMENT ProxyPullSupplier EMPTY>
```

This example is mostly placeholders. One can put values of each <!Element> in a separate file. An <!ENTITY ... > signifies a container for ProxyPushConsumer data.

Declaring Element Type: Persistent

Here are some basic points one might get from brainstorming about the Persistent Object Service:

- Handles object over time
- Components
  - ❏ Client
  - ❏ Persistent Object (PO) and Identifier (PID)
  - ❏ Persistent Object Manager (POM)
  - ❏ Persistent Data Service (PDS)
  - ❏ Database or flat file
  - ❏ Protocol
- Controlling methods
  - ❏ Connection/disconnect
  - ❏ Store/restore
- Twenty-eight interfaces
  - ❏ PID
    - ● PID_DB
    - ● PID_SQLDB
    - ● PID_OODB
    - ● PIDFactory
  - ❏ PO
    - ● POFactory
  - ❏ SD (Synchronized Data)

❑ PDS
- ● PID_DA
- ● DAObject
- ● DAObjectFactory
- ● DAObjectFactoryFinder
- ● PDS_DA
- ● DynamicAttributeAccess
- ● PDS_ClusteredDA

❑ POM

❑ Protocol

❑ Datastore
- ● UserEnvironment
- ● Connection
- ● ConnectionFactory
- ● Cursor
- ● CursorFactory
- ● PID_CLI (call level interface)
- ● Datastore_CLI

❑ Object

❑ DDO (Dynamic Data Object)

■ Non-CORBA interfaces can be used.

```
<- - Persistent Service has 9 primary interfaces. - ->
<- - 19 secondary interfaces - ->
<- - Consider the use of non-CORBA interfaces - ->
<!ELEMENT persistent (PID, …, DDO)>
<!ELEMENT PID EMPTY>
<!ELEMENT PO EMPTY>
```

One must consider in the design if non-CORBA interfaces are used. If a non-CORBA interface is used, XML does permit the calling of external entities. One needs to consider in the original design only those interfaces that require input variables.

Declaring Element Type: LifeCycle

Here are some basic points one might get from brainstorming about the Life Cycle Service:

- Defines conventions for object
  - ❑ Creating
  - ❑ Deleting
  - ❑ Copying
  - ❑ Moving
- Twenty interfaces including:
  - ❑ DocFactory (create)
  - ❑ LifeCycleObject (copy or move)
  - ❑ FactoryFinder (copy or move)
  - ❑ GenericFactory (copy or move)
  - ❑ CosCompoundLifeCycle::Operations
  - ❑ CosCompoundLifeCycle::Node
  - ❑ CosCompoundLifeCycle::Role
  - ❑ CosCompoundLifeCycle::Relationship
- There are 12 additional interfaces in the CosCompoundLifeCycle module.
- Need to define differences between life cycle and compound life cycle

```
<- - LifeCycle Service has 4 interfaces. - ->
<- - Compound Life Cycle (CLC) has 4 key interfaces - ->
<- - CLC also has 12 other interfaces - ->
<!ELEMENT lifecycle (DocFactory, …,)>
<!ELEMENT DocFactory EMPTY>
```

For the design of a DTD for LifeCycle it is important to notice there is a "regular" life cycle and there is a compound life cycle. One should also consider how one would resolve functionality, that is, DocFactory only creates objects, while the other three key interfaces can be used for copying and moving objects.

Declaring Element Type: Concurrency

Here are some basic points one might get from brainstorming about the Concurrency Control Service:

- Better name would be Lock Manager
- Four interfaces
  - ❏ LockSet
  - ❏ LockSetFactory
  - ❏ TransactionalLockSet
  - ❏ LockCoordinator
- Locks are on or off
- Lock granularity
  - ❏ Coarse
  - ❏ Fine
- Lock modes
  - ❏ Read
  - ❏ Write
  - ❏ Upgrade
  - ❏ Intention read
  - ❏ Intention write
- Interfaces support operations and clients that are:
  - ❏ Transactional
  - ❏ Non-transactional
- Services can be:
  - ❏ Implicit
  - ❏ Explicit
- Each lock has a single client and a single resource association.

```
<- - Concurrency Control Service has 4 interfaces. - ->
<!ELEMENT concurrency (LockSet, …, LockCoordinator)>
<!ELEMENT LockSet EMPTY)>
<!ATTLIST LockSet
        state (off | lock_mode) "lock_mode"
        lock_mode (read | write | |upgrade | intention_read |
                   intention_write) "read">
<!ELEMENT LockSetFactory EMPTY>
<!ELEMENT TransactionalLockSet EMPTY>
<!ELEMENT LockCoordinator EMPTY>
```

Notice that instead of lock states of "on" and "off," the states are "lock_mode" and "off." This declaration enables one to relate to a variable from CORBA coding.

Declaring Element Type: Externalization

Here are some basic points one might get from brainstorming about the Externalization Service:

- Handles the way of getting data into and out of a component.
- Defines protocols and conventions for achieving goals.
- Protocol definitions for views of:
  - ❏ Client
  - ❏ Object
  - ❏ Stream
- Six major interfaces
  - ❏ Stream (client)
    - StreamFactory
  - ❏ StreamIO (object)
  - ❏ Streamable (stream)
    - StreamableFactory
  - ❏ Node (stream)
  - ❏ Role (stream)
  - ❏ Relationship (stream)
    - PropagationCriteriaFactory
    - ContainsRole
    - ContainedInRole
    - ReferencesRole
    - ReferencedByRole
- Interfaces from Relationship and Life Cycle Services are used in processing

```
<- - Externalization Service has 6 major interfaces. - ->
<- - Has a number of secondary interfaces - ->
<- - Uses interfaces from Relationship and Life Cycle Services - ->
<!ELEMENT externalization (Stream, …, Relationship)>
<!ELEMENT LockSetFactory EMPTY>
```

Any DTD or any part of a DTD design for Externalization needs to think about the use of three views of the protocols and conventions that are used to achieve expected goals. These views are client, object, and stream. It is also important to consider what interfaces are used to handle each view. This example is a placeholder for further development.

Declaring Element Type: Relationship

Here are some basic points one might get from brainstorming about the
Relationship Service:

■ Relationships can be:
  ❑ One-to-one
  ❑ One-to-many
■ Provides dynamic relationships
■ Categories
  ❑ Cardinality
  ❑ Degree
  ❑ Roles
  ❑ Semantic
  ❑ Types
■ Kinds of objects
  ❑ Roles
  ❑ Relationships
■ Levels of service
  ❑ Base
  ❑ Graph
  ❑ Specific
■ Two core interfaces
  ❑ Relationship
  ❑ Role
■ Secondary interfaces (some)
  ❑ RelationshipFactory
  ❑ RoleFactory
  ❑ RelationshipIterator
■ Need to have clear definitions of relationships and roles for design

```
<- - Relationship Service has two major interfaces. - ->
<- - Has a number of secondary interfaces - ->
<!ELEMENT relationship (RelationI, RoleI)>
<!ELEMENT RelationI EMPTY>
<!ELEMENT RoleI EMPTY>
```

One needs in this design to distinguish between what is a "relationship" and what is a "role." This example uses RelationI for relationship interface and RoleI for role interface. While there is an abbreviated "name" in each case, these "names" are meaningful for a reader of the markup. Under relationship, one can develop a logical structure based on types of categories, objects, and service levels. Under role, one could include in the structure declarations for secondary interfaces.

Declaring Element Type: Transaction

Here are some basic points one might get from brainstorming about the Transaction Service:

- Manages context directly or indirectly
- Interfaces are:
  - Coordinator
  - Current
  - RecoveryCoordinator
  - Resource
  - SubtransactionAwareResource
  - Synchronization
  - Terminator
  - TransactionalObject
  - TransactionFactory
- Characteristic
  - Atomic
  - Consistent
  - Isolated
  - Durable
- Object types
  - Transactional
    - Client
    - Object
    - Server
  - Recoverable
    - Object
    - Server

- Handling types
  - ❏ Direct/explicit
  - ❏ Direct/implicit
  - ❏ Indirect/explicit
  - ❏ Indirect/implicit
- Application types
  - ❏ Transaction client
  - ❏ Transactional client
  - ❏ Recoverable object
  - ❏ Transactional servers
  - ❏ Recoverable servers

```
<- - Transaction Service has nine interfaces. - ->
<- - Order interfaces by programming use - ->
<!ELEMENT transaction (Current, …, TransactionalObject)>
<!ELEMENT Current EMPTY>
<!ELEMENT TransactionFactory EMPTY>
```

Under Transaction Service one can use characteristics and types to establish specific value types within <!ATTLIST>. This example implies that the interfaces are the second level of the logical structure and third level of the document. The root level, or first level, of the document is the document type, domains. This is a part of the physical structure since it is the document entity, (!DOCTYPE domains>, the ultimate container.

Declaring Element Type: Query

Here are some basic points one might get from brainstorming about the Query Service:

- Enables search by methods other than indexing
- Supports two query languages
  - ❏ SQL-92 Query
  - ❏ OQL-93
- Eight interfaces
  - ❏ CollectionFactory
  - ❏ Collection
  - ❏ Iterator
  - ❏ QueryLanguage

❑ QueryEvaluator
❑ QueryableCollection
❑ QueryManager
❑ Query
■ Used with Object Collections Service
■ Supports top-level querying
■ Some types of query collection that can be used
❑ Equality
❑ Key
❑ Ordered (sort or sequential)

```
<- - Query Service has eight interfaces. - ->
<!ELEMENT query (CollectionFactory, …, Query)>
<- - creates collections - ->
<!ELEMENT CollectionFactory EMPTY>
<- - aggregates objects - ->
<!ELEMENT Collection EMPTY>
<- - iterates over collections - ->
<!ELEMENT Iterator EMPTY>
<- - represents query language types - ->
<!ELEMENT QueryLanguage EMPTY>
<- - evaluates query predicates - ->
<- - executes query operations - ->
<!ELEMENT QueryEvaluator EMPTY>
<- - represent query scope and result - ->
<!ELEMENT QueryableCollection EMPTY>
<- - creates query objects - ->
<- - processes queries - ->
<!ELEMENT QueryManager EMPTY>
<- - represents queries - ->
<!ELEMENT Query EMPTY>
```

How one designs XML markup, the DTD, is based on three factors. The first factor is what type of query language is used and its associated "jargon." The second factor is types of queries that are to be used. The final factor is the level to which one wants to integrate their query abilities into CORBAservices.

Declaring Element Type: Licensing

Here are some basic points one might get from brainstorming about the Licensing Service:

- Assists in controlling intellectual property
- Two interfaces
  - ❏ LicenseServiceManager
  - ❏ ProductSpecificLicenseService
- Controls supported
  - ❏ Consumer
    - ● Assignment
    - ● Reservation
  - ❏ Time
    - ● Expiration
    - ● Duration
  - ❏ Value mapping

```
<- - Licensing Service has two interfaces. - ->
<- - Shorten names of interfaces - ->
<!ELEMENT licensing (License, Product)>
<- - full name LicenseServiceManager - ->
<!ELEMENT License EMPTY>
<- - full name ProductSpecificLicenseService - ->
<!ELEMENT Product EMPTY>
```

While the brainstorming for Licensing appears to be one of the shortest of all done here, that does not mean it is the easiest. One needs to reflect on local legal conditions for each involved product. Notice the active word is "each." Design for Licensing should be done on a general level. While the licensing for two products (objects) may have the appearance of being the same, they may only be similar.

Declaring Element Type: Property

Here are some basic points one might get from brainstorming about the Property Service:

- An object can store information on another object.
- Property has a name and value

- Supports:
  - ❑ Defining
  - ❑ Deleting
  - ❑ Enumerating
  - ❑ Checking
- Property modes
  - ❑ Normal
  - ❑ Readonly
  - ❑ Fixed_Normal
  - ❑ Fixed_Readonly
  - ❑ Undefined
- Interfaces that must be supported
  - ❑ PropertySet
  - ❑ PropertySetDef
- Other interfaces
  - ❑ PropertiesIterator
  - ❑ PropertyNamesIterator
  - ❑ PropertySetFactory
  - ❑ PropertySetDefFactory

```
<- - Property Service has two interfaces that must be supported - ->
<- - Has four other interfaces - ->
<!ELEMENT property (Set, SetDef)>
<- - full name is PropertySet - ->
<- - supports a set of properties - ->
<!ELEMENT Set EMPTY>
<- - full name is PropertySetDef - ->
<- - exposes a property's characteristics (metadata) - ->
<!ELEMENT SetDef EMPTY>
```

In this design two ideas must be taken into account. The first is an answer to the question, "Why should information from an object be stored with another object?" The second idea is that any property has a name and a value. One needs also to determine how the four functions (creating, deleting, enumerating, and checking) are implemented in the basic DTD design.

Declaring Element Type: Time

Here are some basic points one might get from brainstorming about the Time Service:

- Synchronizes events
- Six interfaces
    - ❏ TimeService
    - ❏ TimeEventService
    - ❏ TIO (Time Interval Object)
    - ❏ UTO (Universal Time Object)
    - ❏ TimerEventHandler
    - ❏ TimerEventService
- Uses Greenwich Mean Time
- Base date of October 15, 1582 (Gregorian calendar)
- Conformance points
    - ❏ Basic Time Service
    - ❏ Timer Event Service
- Authorized personnel can only set time.
- Implementation requires how time values for time synchronization are protected while they are transmitted over a network. (Secure is either equal to "yes" or "no".)

```
<- - Time Service has two major service interfaces - ->
<- - Has four other interfaces - ->
<- -transmission secure state - ->
<!ELEMENT time EMPTY>
<!ATTLIST time  state (yes | no) "yes">
```

Part **III**

When integrating this service into your system, one must comprehend the significance of the two rules that define time. The base date is October 15, 1582 (Gregorian calendar). The base time is Greenwich Mean Time. The question that needs to be asked about base time is "What is the effect of daylight savings time?"

Note: When Pope Gregory XIII proclaimed the Gregorian calendar to be the calendar of the Church it was October 15, 1582 (Gregorian calendar), while the prior day was October 4, 1582 (Julian calendar). The Gregorian calendar did not become the dating standard in Europe until the time of the Communist Revolution.

Declaring Element Type: Security

The Security Service impacts all of the other services, including those defined and those yet to be defined. Because of its importance, Chapter 13 details more on security than the information given here for any other service discussed.

Declaring Element Type: Trader

Here are some basic points one might get from brainstorming about the Object Trader Service:

- Provides an object matchmaking service
- Offer types
  - ❏ Potential
  - ❏ Considered
  - ❏ Matched
  - ❏ Ordered
  - ❏ Returned
- Three core interfaces
  - ❏ DynamicPropEval
  - ❏ ServiceTypeRepository
  - ❏ TraderComponents
- TradeComponents has a series of interfaces based on the functions:
  - ❏ Lookup
  - ❏ Register
  - ❏ Link
  - ❏ Proxy
  - ❏ Admin
- Property mode attributes
  - ❏ Mandatory

- ❏ Readonly
- ■ Preference types
  - ❏ Max expression
  - ❏ Min expression
  - ❏ With expression
  - ❏ Random
  - ❏ First
- ■ Conformance is by interface rather than by service.

```
<- - Trading Object Service has three major service interfaces - ->
<- - Has a large number of interfaces based on functionality - ->
<!ELEMENT trading EMPTY>
<!ELEMENT type (potential | considered | matched | ordered | returned)
              "potential">
<!ELEMENT function (lookup | register | link | proxy | admin) "lookup">
<!ELEMENT preference (max | min | with | random | first) 'with'>
```

The keys for developing a design for the Object Trader Service are types of offers and functionality, in particular those of the TraderComponents Interface. This example shows how to use "or" (|) in <!ELEMENT>. The default is the value within the double quotation marks or the single quotation marks, such as "potential" or 'with.'

Declaring Element Type: Collections

Here are some basic points one might get from brainstorming about the Object Collections Service:

- ■ Manipulates a group of objects as one
- ■ Some collection properties
  - ❏ Unordered
    - ● Unique
      - ○ Map
      - ○ KeySet
      - ○ Set
    - ● Multiple
      - ○ Relation
      - ○ KeyBag
      - ○ Bag
      - ○ Heap

- ❏ Ordered
  - ● Sorted
    - ○ Unique
      - ➤ Sorted Map
      - ➤ Key Sorted Set
      - ➤ SortedSet
    - ○ Multiple
      - ➤ Sorted Relation
      - ➤ Key SortedBag
      - ➤ Sorted Bag
  - ● Sequential
    - ○ Multiple
      - ➤ Equality Sequence
      - ➤ Sequence
- ■ Operation types
  - ❏ Creating
  - ❏ Adding
  - ❏ Removing
  - ❏ Replacing
  - ❏ Retrieving
  - ❏ Inquiring
- ■ Client selects a collection interface that offers grouping properties that match needs.
  - ❏ Collection
  - ❏ OrderedCollection
  - ❏ KeyCollection
  - ❏ EqualityCollection
  - ❏ SortedCollection
  - ❏ SequentialCollection
  - ❏ EqualitySequentialCollection
  - ❏ EqualityKeyCollection
  - ❏ KeySortedCollection
  - ❏ EqualityKeySortedCollection
- ■ There is a series of interfaces based on functions.
  - ❏ Operations
  - ❏ Command

    ❏ Comparator
- There are 32 interfaces for concrete collections and their factories.
- There are ten interfaces for restricted access collections and their factories.
- There are 11 iterator interfaces.
- There are a total of 67 Object Collections interfaces.
- Required element information
  - ❏ How to do comparisons
  - ❏ How to test equality
  - ❏ How to do checking

The design for <!ELEMENT collections (…) > should be within the grouping interfaces such as follows:

```
<!ELEMENT collection (…) >
<!ELEMENT Collection (yes | no) "yes" >
<!ELEMENT OrderedCollection (yes | no) "no" >
…
<!ELEMENT EqualityKeySortedCollection (yes | no) "no" >
```

The fact there are 67 Object Collections interfaces says something about design difficulties for this service. The example implies that use of "yes" and "no" for establishing the availability of each property for defining collections may be a potential design that can be used.

Designing an XML DTD for the Security Service

Included in This Chapter:

- ❑ Speaking "Policy"
- ❑ Identifying Attributes
- ❑ Using the Application Developer's Interfaces
- ❑ Using the Administrator's Interfaces
- ❑ Using the Implementor's Interfaces
- ❑ Planning an XML Security Service DTD System
- ❑ Guidelines for Developing DTDs for Security

There is only one security principle; everything else is commentary. The highest level of security is the weakest link in the system.

Within CORBA *security* is the mechanism or policy[1] infrastructure that defines and enforces access control on objects and their constituents. In a broader sense the security mechanism authenticates and validates a user's identification and protects a system's integrity that is its communication component, requests and responses. This mechanism should be as

---

[1] The OMG security specification is based on the implementation of a "local" security policy. The framework is generic. This policy serves as a framework for a security reference model. Developers, administrators, and implementors determine the implementation result.

transparent to the client as possible. Simply stated, the key functions of security are:

- Access control
- Administration
- Auditing
- Authentication
- Authorization
- Identification
- Non-repudiation
- Secure communication

Note: These eight functions need to be considered in the design of any security DTD. The methodology focus with CORBA is on its interfaces.

What should be the design goals of a CORBA security service? This list sounds like the reasons for the design goals or principles of XML. They are as follows:

- Accountability
- Confidentiality
- Consistency
- Flexibility
  - ❏ Access control
  - ❏ Audit policy
  - ❏ Profiles
- Interoperability
- Minimal performance overhead
- Object-oriented
- Portability
- Scalability
- Simplicity
- Technologically neutral
- Usability
  - ❏ Administrators

❑ Developers

❑ End users

In the context of defining functions and establishing goals for security, one needs to identify various types of attributes. Three broad attribute types are:

■ Public

■ Authenticated

■ Delegated

Because of the importance of security, extensive development is going on in CORBAservices, CORBAfacilities, and domains. Security is briefly alluded to in Chapters 11 and 14. Security is a fundamental component of the CORBA infrastructure.

Besides considering the importance of CORBA interfaces and related attributes, design principles, and functions for security, there are other items one should put in the design. They include:

■ Security associations

■ Server implications

The key to security association is trust. There needs to be a *persistent* method for security between a client and a target object. Besides trust, there also need to be methodologies for establishing credentials and a protected context.

Note: *Persistent* is the functionality that handles objects over time. It is a transtemporal and transcending function.

Each server style has its implications for the degree of security possible. Its object adapter determines the server style. In the design of the CORBA Security Service, one needs to look at the functionality of least four server types:

■ Shared

■ Unshared

■ Per method

■ Persistent

To design and develop an XML DTD[2] that reflects key security functionality and CORBA implementation of a security service, one must be knowledgeable of two items:

■ Fundamental security attributes
■ CORBA Security Service interfaces

The interfaces are for three types of people:

■ Administrator
■ Application developer
■ Implementor

This chapter closes with guidelines for designing an XML DTD system for a CORBA security service. Local factors determine an actual model.

Speaking "Policy"

One can more easily comprehend the CORBA security infrastructure when one can define the basic functionality of each policy type. Policy applies to the objects, while security technology focuses on how to implement the functionality.

Client invocation access	The access decision is either yes or no. Does the client have the right to invoke the access?
Target invocation access	The access decision is either yes or no. Does the target have the right to do this invocation?
Application access	Domain manager determines the granularity of access.
Client invocation audit	The nature of the event and criteria determines policy control for the client.
Target invocation audit	The nature of the event and criteria determines policy control for the target.
Application audit	The application may determine policy control rather than the security domain.
Delegation	The nature or type of delegating determines policy control. Delegation includes the roles and responsibilities of intermediaries.

---

2   While "an XML DTD" is used here perhaps it is more practical to use the phrase "an XML DTD system" to further enhance the protection of the security infrastructure.

Client secure invocation	This invocation's determination includes resolutions for confidentiality, integrity, and privacy. It also invokes authentication for the client.
Target secure invocation	This invocation's determination includes resolutions for confidentiality, integrity, and privacy. It also invokes authentication for the target.
Non-repudiation	This optional facility provides evidence of acts by an application in a form that cannot be repudiated at a later time.
Construction	This policy controls the creation of domains.

Identifying Attributes

There is no simple list of attributes for a security service because of local goals and legacy hardware and software. Perhaps there are some common attributes or attribute types. A common attribute would be a client's identification. A common attribute type would be level of trust. One might define an attribute as a specific characteristic with a specific instance. An attribute type might be defined as a generally characteristic with its own secondary characteristics. One general thinks of read, write, and read-write levels of protection, but perhaps there are different levels of protection such as ones for e-mail and those for chat.

The obvious area to look at for attributes is the access control function. There may be three types of access control attributes:

■ Privilege
■ Control
■ Rights

Some of the privilege attributes are:

■ Client's identification
■ Client's function(s) or role(s)
■ Client's organizational affiliation(s)
■ Client's clearance level
■ Client's operational level

Some of the control attributes are:

■ Control list types

■ Information labels

■ Sharing capabilities

Rights can be established on:

■ Individual basis

■ Group basis

■ Functional basis

■ Operational basis

The second area for identifying attributes is for the auditing function. Auditing can be divided into broad categories: system and application. An audit structure is usually called a policy. Auditing can involve logging events, alerts, or alarms. An audit invocation can include types of:

■ Object

■ Operation

■ Event

■ State (success or failure)

The third area for identifying attributes is the delegation function. At least two types of delegation schema are privilege and reference. Delegation can involve four objects:

■ Initiator

■ Invoker

■ Intermediary

■ Receptor

When considering the privilege delegation, there are two concepts that have to be considered: control type and delegation type. Control type comes in three flavors:

■ Privileges delegated

■ Target restrictions

■ Privileges used

The delegation types that are used by CORBA security interfaces include:

■ None

■ Simple

- Composite
- Combined
- Trace
- Time control

The fourth area for identifying attributes is the non-repudiation function. This function makes users accountable for their actions. CORBA uses application control rather than object invocation. The three key components of non-repudiation are:

- Evidence
  - ❏ Time
  - ❏ Date
  - ❏ Data origin
  - ❏ Data integrity
  - ❏ Proof of creation
  - ❏ Proof of reception
- Action or event type
- Action or event parameters

Using the Application Developer's Interfaces

The interfaces used by the application developer are based on the developer's responsible for business objects in the system. Because in many cases application security is transparent to the developer, the ORB security services are based on automatic object invocation. Some of the items included in the CORBA security model are:

- Specified quality of protection
- Independent auditing
- Attributes definitions for:
  - ❏ Authentication
  - ❏ Privilege
  - ❏ Rights
  - ❏ Access control

Interfaces for application developer include for:

- The ORB
- Credentials

Part III

- Audit decision
- Audit channel
- Access decision
- Delegation
- Non-repudiation

However, for designing an XML DTD, the important requirement is knowledge about the "gets," "sets," "overrides," and type definitions. It is the parameter requirements that are significant.

There are four important types used in these interfaces. They are used in developing local security policies and mechanism. They are as follows:

- Service Options for Service Type Security
  - ❑ SecurityLevel1 = 1
  - ❑ SecurityLevel2 = 2
  - ❑ NonRepudiation = 3
  - ❑ SecurityORBServiceReady = 4
  - ❑ SecurityServiceReady = 5
  - ❑ ReplaceORBServices = 6
  - ❑ ReplaceSecurityServices = 7
  - ❑ StandardSecureInteroperability = 8
  - ❑ DCESecureInteroperability = 9
- Attributes Types for Privilege Attributes
  - ❑ Public = 1
  - ❑ AccessId = 2
  - ❑ PrimaryGroupId = 3
  - ❑ GroupId = 4
  - ❑ Role = 5
  - ❑ AttributeSet = 6
  - ❑ Clearance = 7
  - ❑ Capability = 8
- Association Options for Context Initialization
  - ❑ NoProtection = 1
  - ❑ Integrity = 2
  - ❑ Confidentiality = 4
  - ❑ DetectReplay = 8
  - ❑ DetectMisordering = 16

❑ EstablishTrustInTarget = 32
❑ EstablishTrustInClient = 64
■ Selector Types for Audit Events
❑ InterfaceRef =1
❑ ObjectRef = 2
❑ Operation = 3
❑ Initiator = 4
❑ SuccessFailure = 5
❑ Time = 6

Note: There are other values that also need to be considered.

The interface ORB has two parameters for "in" and "out" information. They are:

■ service_type
■ service_information

A Credentials object has four "in" and three "out" attributes. They are:

■ method
■ security_name
■ auth_data
■ privileges
■ creds
■ continuation_data
■ auth_specific_data

For an authentication that requires multiple operations, there are one "in," one "in-out," and two "out" attributes:

■ response_data
■ creds
■ continuation_data
■ auth_specific_data

There are three Boolean attributes (true or false) to set privilege. Two are "in." They are:

■ force_commit

- requested_privileges
- actual_privileges

A client application that is security-aware can perform certain operations to specific security policy. These operations include:

- override_default_credentials
- override_default_QOP
- get_active_credentials
- get_security_features
- get_policy
- get_security_mechanism
- override_default_mechanism
- get_security_names

The Current object represents service-specific state information associated with the current execution context. The information can use one or more of these credential types:

- Invocation
- Own
- Received
- Non-repudiation

The Audit Channel object receives an audit record. The record must contain:

- Event type
- Actor with credentials
- Event-specific data (varies by event type)
- Time

In the delegation chain the intermediate object can do one of three actions. These actions are:

- Delegate credentials to next object in the chain.
- Act for itself.
- Supply privileges from both initiator and self.

Warning: This section highlighted only some of the interface variables and some of their associated variables. These data assist one in creating a modeling process using CORBA data for designing an XML DTD with the document type of *security*.

Using the Administrator's Interfaces

The interfaces to be used by the administrator are based on the policy for user control or management. CORBA permits multiple administrators. The administrator is concerned with administrative groupings. The administrator is responsible for defining the security and privilege attributes for both human and electronic (application) users.

Note: One area of the model that needs development is one for explicit management interfaces.

The key interfaces for an administrator include:

■ Policy
■ DomainManager
■ ConstructionPolicy:Policy
■ Object
■ RequiredRights
■ AccessPolicy
■ DomainAccessPolicy

As with the developer, the important requirement for the administrator is knowledge about the "gets," "sets," and attributes. The first step is actually defining the attributes of the administrator.

The domain manager provides mechanisms for handling security relationships and policies. It involves two important parameters. They are:

■ policy_type
■ object_type

Invocation security policies are automatically enforced for four types of invocations:

■ Access
■ Audit

- Delegation
- Secure

Note: There is one standard interface for application access, but not one for administration.

The get_required_rights operation has three "in" and two "out" attributes. They are:

- obj
- operation_name
- interface_name
- rights
- rights_combination

Note: The last four are used in the set_required_rights.

There are three standard rights in CORBA:

- "g" (get)
- "s" (set)
- "m" (manage)

They are used in the form corba:gsm with one or more as a suffix.

There are four attributes for three DomainAccessPolicy operations, grant_rights, revoke_rights, and replace_rights. They are:

- priv_attr
- del_state
- rights_family
- rights

The retrieve rights operation uses the first three attributes.

The four audit selectors (set, clear, replace, and get) have the same three attributes. They are:

- object_type
- events
- selectors

There are attributes for other operations such as object associations, invocation delegation, and evidence (non-repudiation).

Warning: This section highlighted only some of the interface variables and some of their associated variables. These data assist one in creating a modeling process using CORBA data for designing an XML DTD with the document type of *security*.

Using the Implementor's Interfaces

There are three actions an implementor must do to have a secure object system:

- Develop an ORB.
- Develop other associated services and facilities.
- Develop the security services required to provide expected features.

The implementor is concerned with such items as protection boundaries, local security requirements, and credentials.

The key type of interfaces of interest to an implementor is the interceptor. Interceptors include those for the:

- Request-level
- Message-level

The primary parameters an implementor would be interested in, as far as XML DTD design is involved, are those that establish context.

When working with implementor interfaces, there are two important words to remember: generic and context. The generic concept is represented by such operations as get_policy and get_credentials. The attributes init_security_context and accept_security_context can illustrate the content concept.

The init_security_context operation initiates a security association with the target. There are eight "in" and two "out" attributes. They are:

- creds_list
- target_security_name
- target
- delegation_mode

- association_mode
- mechanism
- mech_data
- chan_bindings
- security_token
- security_context

The accept_security_context operation seeks to get an acceptance from the target for a security association with the client. There are three "in" and two "out" attributes. They are:

- creds_list
- chan_bindings
- in_token
- out_token
- security_context

Besides the attributes listed above, there are attributes for such objects as:

- Security Context
- Access Decision
- Audit Decision
- Audit Channel

Warning: This section highlighted only some of the interface variables and some of their associated variables. These data assist one in creating a modeling process using CORBA data for designing an XML DTD with the document type of *security*.

Planning an XML Security Service DTD System

Based on the CORBA Specification, there are three views or users of the CORBA security infrastructure. They are developers, administrators, and implementors. There are also at least ten activities that these users need to consider in the implementation of a CORBA security service. They are:

- Associating client and target through an ORB.
- Identifying access control decision points.
- Defining the client's privilege attributes (a principal).
- Defining the target's control attributes.

- Defining the privileges or controls of any intermediaries.
- Establishing policy domains.
- Identifying the role of each domain manager.
- Delegating operations to any external security mechanism.
- Determining the role and impact of the Object Transaction Service (OTS).
- Implementing security defaults.

When one gets ready to develop an XML DTD that assists in an integration of XML, CORBA, and the legacy environment, one must consider a number of issues:

- What are the criteria for using an object-oriented programming language such as Java in designing and developing this integration?
- Acknowledge that the ORB in and of itself offers minimal security and there needs to be an infrastructure that establishes local goals for a perceived secure level.
- Identify all the values in the CORBA Specification for a Security ORB with its associated interfaces and operations.
- Consider the design proposal that the "gets," "sets," etc., are a potential way of designing the DTD.
- What should be the level of detail of the XML DTD for designing a CORBA Security ORB?
- Has one accounted for all the key functions of security such as confidentiality and accountability?
- Has one ensured that the five key security services have been implemented in the DTD design?
  - ❑ Authentication
  - ❑ Authorization
  - ❑ Confidentiality
  - ❑ Integrity
  - ❑ Non-repudiation
- Has the DTD design established the places of the client and target objects?
- Has the DTD design considered adequately all privilege and control attributes?
- Has the DTD design taken into account the delegation roles of the initiator, intermediaries, and final target?

- Has there been a review of the differences between Level One and Level Two security?
- Have all the criteria of the 11 security policies of the ORB been evaluated as to how they affect the local security infrastructure?
  - ❏ Application accesses and audits
  - ❏ Client and target invocation accesses
  - ❏ Client and target invocation audits
  - ❏ Client and target secure invocations
  - ❏ Construction
  - ❏ Delegation
  - ❏ Non-repudiation
- Have the operations of the request and message interceptors been considered in the design?
- Has the place of families (group with mutual characteristics) been determined?
- Have data types been identified that are necessary for developing each of the services?
- Have the developmental steps been defined for each type of user—the application developer, the administrator, and the implementor?
- Can there be a common DTD template that can be used by all three user types?

These seventeen issues reflect that the designing of an XML DTD for Security Services may not be an easy task. In fact, the last question may be the key design question. Should there be only one DTD? That answer is perhaps. It can be no because there are different document types as established in other chapters. There can be different views of the same data. The working word is <u>data</u>, not <u>text</u>. Each individual must work out her or his own DTD; however, there may be a common process. The detail evolves out of one's XML experience, security infrastructure experience, and needs. Perhaps in a later evolution in knowledge of CORBA and of XML implications there can be an answer of yes.

Guidelines for Developing DTDs for Security

Guidelines are given here rather than specific examples because the final set of XML DTDs should be based on local declarations. Also, to further ensure security it is recognized that hackers have accessed systems because someone used examples from some documentation verbatim.

Perhaps one needs to consider an "XML DTD system" rather that just a single DTD or a DTD each for development, administration, and implementation. The specification may have established separate interfaces for each of these three areas; however, the ultimate goal is to have an integrated security policy.

The first step might be to establish a "root DTD" that has a set of entity declarations for each policy type. These policy types are found in module CORBA enumerated under PolicyType (policy types are listed earlier in this chapter). As appropriate, one could comment out any policy type not a part of one's view.

The second step would be to identify associated interfaces and their variables by policy type. There are sections in this chapter that highlight some of these interfaces and variables for each user.

The third step is to develop DTDs according to the user's responsibilities.

■ Application Developer: handles business objects in the system.

■ Administrator: handles user control or management.

■ Implementor: handles such activities as boundary definitions, security requirements, and credentials.

The fourth step is to create DTDs for each interface as an element and use attribute lists to declare the variables.

The fifth step is the addition of any data relevant to the user's responsibilities and refinements for local security policy. This one includes the responsibilities of any domain managers.

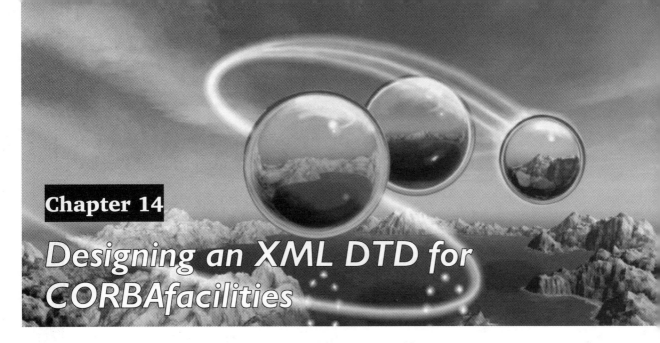

Chapter 14

Designing an XML DTD for CORBAfacilities

Included in This Chapter:

- ❏ Declaring the Document Type: Facilities
- ❏ Declaring Element Type: UserIf
- ❏ Declaring Element Type: Information
- ❏ Declaring Element Type: Systems
- ❏ Declaring Element Type: Task
- ❏ Declaring Element Type: Imagery
- ❏ Declaring Element Type: InfoSuper
- ❏ Declaring Element Type: Manufacturing
- ❏ Declaring Element Type: Simulation
- ❏ Declaring Element Type: OAGI
- ❏ Declaring Element Type: Accounting
- ❏ Declaring Element Type: AppDev
- ❏ Declaring Element Type: Mapping

This chapter declares some XML elements and attribute lists for some of the 12 facilities that make up CORBAfacilities based on information from Chapter 9 and the CORBAfacilities: Common Facilities Architecture V4.0 November 1995 Specification. The premise here is that an XML document can handle data and that one uses the concepts developed for CORBAfacilities as a starting point for eventual CORBA/XML integration. This chapter is basically a "what-if" one rather than a "how-to" chapter.

The XML examples for CORBAfacilities are broadly structured using the interfaces for declaring XML elements. The information given here is a set of brainstorming sessions looking at the issue of CORBA/XML integration. It is recognized that a number of applications would be required to complete this integration.

Also see Chapter 11 (Domains) and Chapter 12 (Services) for similar considerations. This chapter looks at the potential of CORBAfacilities and the potential use of XML with various facilities.

Declaring the Document Type: Facilities

The first two declarations required are an XML declaration (Rule 23) and a document type declaration (Rule 28). Also included at this point is the element type declaration (Rule 39) for facilities. Everything else goes between the start of the document type declaration and the end "]>". This document of facilities says that a full set of CORBAfacilities includes the specified features (interfaces). Also included are the appropriate attributes, entities, and notations. All of these declarations constitute the document type definition (DTD).

```
<?xml version="1.0">
<DOCTYPE facilities [
<!ELEMENT facilities (rendering, … , mapping)>
]<
```

The data that goes within the ellipsis are the other CORBAfacilities. This chapter looks at both horizontal and vertical CORBAfacilities. There are various DTD design considerations as creating two document types facilities-hor and facilities-ver. This design is one possibility with the facilities given sequentially as in the Specification.

Some of the facility names are changed for ease of markup, such as rendering for Rendering Management. The 12 facilities as used in this chapter are as follows:

- UserIf (User Interface Common Facility)
- Information (Information Management Common Facility)
- Systems (System Management Common Facility)

- Task (Task Management Common Facility)
- Imagery
- InfoSuper (Information Superhighways)
- Manufacturing
- Simulation (Distributed Simulation)
- OAGI (Oil and Gas Industry Exploration and Production)
- Accounting
- AppDev (Application Development)
- Mapping

Note: The two special CORBAfacilities, Internationalization and Security, are not discussed in this chapter.

Each of the following 12 sections begins with a kind of brainstorming of each facility based on information from Chapter 9 and from the CORBAfacilities Specification. The focus of the "brainstorming" is to establish a "draft" framework of the logical structure of each facility. This, in turn, is the basis for developing a logical XML structure and in some cases an enhanced physical structure for a facility. There is one necessary entity, the document entity.

Warning: The information given here should <u>NOT</u> be considered complete. It is ideas, or even better, it is speculations for relating concepts from CORBA with those from XML. These declarations are commented to reflect ideas for design.

Declaring Element Type: UserIf

Here are some basic points one might get from brainstorming about the User Interface Facility:

- Five major areas
  - ❏ Rendering Management
  - ❏ Compound Presentation
  - ❏ User Support
  - ❏ Desktop Management

- ❏ Scripting
- ■ Rendering concerns
  - ❏ Window management
  - ❏ User interface objects
  - ❏ Dialogue objects
  - ❏ Device abstractions
- ■ Presentation concerns
  - ❏ Geometry management
  - ❏ Event distribution (human interface)
  - ❏ Controls (human interface)
  - ❏ Rendering management
- ■ User support concerns
  - ❏ Annotating
  - ❏ Graphic functions
  - ❏ Spreadsheet functions
  - ❏ Versioning
- ■ Desktop concerns
  - ❏ Information issues
    - ● Aggregations (hierarchies)
    - ● Versions (evolution)
    - ● Configurations (consistency)
  - ❏ Tools
    - ● Editors
    - ● Browsers
    - ● System tools
    - ● Hardware tools
  - ❏ Operational tasks

With these brainstorming ideas and other data from the Specification, one can begin to declare the <!ELEMENT UserIf>.

```
<- - Five areas - ->
<!ELEMENT UserIf (rendering, presentation, support, desktop, scripting)
<!ELEMENT rendering EMPTY>
<!ATTLIST rendering
        winmgt CDATA #REQUIRED
        classlib CDATA #REQUIRED
        dialogobj CDATA #REQUIRED
```

```
                indevice CDATA #REQUIRED
                outdevice CDATA #REQUIRED >
<!ELEMENT presentation EMPTY>
<!ATTLIST presentation
        geometry CDATA #REQUIRED
        eventif CDATA #REQUIRED
        shareif method (menu | palette | button | other) "menu"
        manager CDATA #REQUIRED >
<!ELEMENT support EMPTY>
<!ATTLIST support
        function ftype (help | speller | grammar | other) "other" >
<!ELEMENT desktop EMPTY>
<!ATTLIST desktop
        info itype (agg | ver | config) "agg"
        tool type (editor | browser | system | hardware) "system"
        task CDATA #REQUIRED >
<!ELEMENT scripting EMPTY>
```

The EMPTY content specification type is used to develop a logical framework for a facility. The ATTLIST declarations are used to establish types of content, values, attributes, and placeholders for applications.

This is a broad sweep of the possibilities for the User Interface Facility. Where CDATA is used perhaps is the location for identifying an applications and its location. Another area to be expanded is Desktop Management and its functions.

Declaring Element Type: Information

Here are some basic points one might get from brainstorming about the Information Management Facility:

- Four areas of interest
  - ❑ Modeling
  - ❑ Storage
  - ❑ Information interchange
  - ❑ Information exchange
- Modeling areas
  - ❑ Object interfaces
  - ❑ Service interfaces
  - ❑ Object relationships
  - ❑ Atomic data types

- Storage focuses
  - ❏ Application development
  - ❏ Data warehousing
  - ❏ Systems management
- Retrieval transactions
  - ❏ Initialization
  - ❏ Search
  - ❏ Retrieve
  - ❏ Access control
  - ❏ Termination
- Information interchange could almost be considered a facility unto itself.
  - ❏ Compound interchange
    - ● Binding
    - ● Annotation
    - ● Conversion
    - ● Exchange
    - ● Linking
    - ● Reference storage
  - ❏ Data interchange
    - ● Domain-specific object representations
    - ● Formatted data
    - ● Bulk data transfer
    - ● Structured data
    - ● Legacy data
- Information exchange
  - ❏ Infrastructure
  - ❏ Enabling technology
  - ❏ Semantics
  - ❏ Support
  - ❏ Mediated information exchange
    - ● Content language
    - ● Vocabulary
    - ● Communication
    - ● Interaction control

- ❑ Data encoding
  - ● Storage media
  - ● Networking protocols
  - ● Programming interfaces
- ❑ Data types
  - ● Compression
  - ● Decompression
  - ● Representation to canonical conversion
  - ● Canonical to representation conversion
- ❑ Quality of service
- ❑ Time manipulation
  - ● Stamping
  - ● Duration
  - ● Range
  - ● Comparison
  - ● Instance manipulation

```
<- - Four areas - ->
<!ELEMENT information (modeling, storage, interchange, exchange)
<!ELEMENT modeling EMPTY >
<- - objif = object interface - ->
<- - svcif = service interface set - ->
<- - objrelation = relationships between objects - ->
<- - datatype = describe exchanged data and atomic types - ->
<- - graphicedit = graphical editor for diagram drawing - ->
<- - datareposdb = persistent data repository for object handling - ->
<- - browser =  capability to see repository contents - ->
<- - datareposapp = application program interface to the repository -
->
<- - typeext = type extension capability for new object types - ->
<- - rptsys = reporting system to support project documentation
standards - ->
<!ATTLIST modeling
        objif CDATA #REQUIRED
        svcif CDATA #REQUIRED
        objrelation CDATA #REQUIRED
        datatype CDATA #REQUIRED
        graphicedit CDATA #REQUIRED
        datareposdb CDATA #REQUIRED
        browser CDATA #REQUIRED
        datareposapp CDATA #REQUIRED
```

```
              typeext CDATA #REQUIRED
              rptsys CDATA #REQUIRED >
<!ELEMENT storage EMPTY >
<- - service types initialization, search, retrieval, - ->
<- - access-control, termination - ->
<!ATTLIST storage
          initialsvc CDATA #REQUIRED
          searchsvc CDATA #REQUIRED
          retlsvc CDATA #REQUIRED
          accesssvc CDATA #REQUIRED
          termsvc CDATA #REQUIRED >
<!ELEMENT interchange (compound, data) >
<- - need attribute list declarations - ->
<!ELEMENT compound EMPTY >
<!ELEMENT data EMPTY>
<!ELEMENT exchange (language, vocabulary, communication, control) >
<- - need attribute list declarations - ->
<!ELEMENT language EMPTY >
<!ELEMENT vocabulary EMPTY >
<!ELEMENT communication EMPTY >
<!ELEMENT control EMPTY >
```

The facility could have an extensive DTD because the information system or information technology environment has such a high level of definition. This example only brushes on possibilities.

Declaring Element Type: Systems

Here are some basic points one might get from brainstorming about the System Management Facility:

■ Eleven facilities
  ❑ User types
  ❑ Policy management
  ❑ Quality of service management
  ❑ Instrumentation
  ❑ Data logging
  ❑ Security management
  ❑ Collection management
  ❑ Instance management
  ❑ Scheduling management

- ❏ Customization
- ❏ Event management
- ■ Types of users
  - ❏ Users
  - ❏ Developers
  - ❏ Service providers
  - ❏ Resource planners
- ■ Quality of service concerns
  - ❏ Availability
  - ❏ Performance
  - ❏ Reliability
  - ❏ Recovery
- ■ Instrumentation issues
  - ❏ Workload
  - ❏ Object allocation
  - ❏ Responsiveness
- ■ Collection types
  - ❏ Queried
  - ❏ Applied
- ■ Event activities
  - ❏ Generation
  - ❏ Registration
  - ❏ Filtration
  - ❏ Aggregation
  - ❏ Notification

```
<- - eleven facilities - ->
<- - see X/Open Resolution 20.6, Interfaces for a Distributed Systems - ->
<- - Management Framework, (IDSMF) - ->
<!ELEMENT systems (user, …, event) >
<- - user types (user, developer, service provider, enterprise) - ->
<- - not limited to these four - ->
<!ELEMENT user EMPTY>
<- - policy management to support policy definition - ->
<- - to support a common interface's application - ->
<- - component creation, deletion, modification - ->
<- - to group resources by policy region - ->
<!ELEMENT policy EMPTY>
```

```
<- - quality of service mgt - ->
<- - concern with availability, performance, reliability, - ->
<- - and recovery - ->
<!ELEMENT QoS EMPTY>
<- - Instrumentation provides for resource-specific data - ->
<- - gathering, managing, and disseminating - ->
<!ELEMENT instrument EMPTY>
<- - Data collection includes Logging and History Management - ->
<- - gathering functionality - ->
<!ELEMENT datalog EMPTY>
<- - Security management - ->
<- - get ideas from Security Facility and Domain - ->
<- - focus is on resource security - ->
<!ELEMENT secmgt EMPTY>
<- - Collection Management requires two-way object references - ->
<- - querying or applying - ->
<!ELEMENT collection EMPTY >
<- - Instance Management provides infrastructure for objects to be - ->
<- - logically associated - ->
<- - support for a single instance and multiple instances - ->
<!ELEMENT instance EMPTY>
<- - Scheduling Management for tasks on a regular basis - ->
<- - Look at the Time Facility - ->
<!ELEMENT schedule EMPTY>
<- - Customization provides for object instances to be extended - ->
<- - while retaining type safety - ->
<- - replacing a piece of hardware through an upgrade - ->
<!ELEMENT customization EMPTY>
<- - Event Management provides for generating, registering, - ->
<- - filtering, aggregating, and forwarding of event notifications - ->
<- -to management applications - ->
<!ELEMENT eventmgt EMPTY>
<- - a placeholder for expansion - ->
<!ELEMENT other EMPTY>
```

This example shows how one could heavily comment a first draft of a
DTD. Also note at the end of the example there is a placeholder for future
expansion.

Declaring Element Type: Task

Here are some basic points one might get from brainstorming about the Task Management Facility:

- Four areas for applications and desktops
  - ❏ Work flows
  - ❏ Agent
  - ❏ Rule management
  - ❏ Automation
- Interacts with the ORB through high-level messaging
- Workflow types
  - ❏ Flows
  - ❏ Long transactions
- Agency
  - ❏ Functions
  - ❏ Agent types (mobile and static)
- Function issues
  - ❏ Agent off-load
  - ❏ Load bookkeeping
- Mobile agent services
  - ❏ Control
  - ❏ Communication
  - ❏ Messaging
- Static agent services
  - ❏ Basic information
  - ❏ Simply query
  - ❏ Multi-response
  - ❏ Assertion
  - ❏ Generation
  - ❏ Capability
  - ❏ Notification
  - ❏ Extension

- Types of extension services
  - ❏ Networking
  - ❏ Facilitation
  - ❏ Database
  - ❏ Adaptation
  - ❏ Error correction
  - ❏ Automatic retransmission
  - ❏ Registration (home and visitor)
  - ❏ Security (encryption and access)
- Rule management considerations
  - ❏ Scripting
  - ❏ Storing
  - ❏ Interpreting
- Automation focuses
  - ❏ Method invocation
  - ❏ Object specifier

```
<- - four facilities - ->
<- - uses many of the services including Event, Life Cycle, Persistent
- ->
<- - Object, Transaction, relation, Query, Concurrency Control - ->
<- - rulemgt =  rule management - ->
<!ELEMENT task (workflow, agent, rulemgt, automation) >
<- - ref.: Workflow Management Coalition, Glossary, August 1994 - ->
<!ELEMENT workflow EMPTY >
<- - ad hoc = coordination-based work flow - ->
<- - pre-defined = production-based work flow - ->
<!ATTLIST workflow
        type (ad hoc | pre-defined) "pre-defined" >
<!ELEMENT agent EMPTY >
<- - ensure you declare all the services - ->
<- - errorcorrect = error correction - ->
<!ATTLIST agent
        mobile (content | communication | messaging | no) "no"
        static (basic | query | multi-response | assertion |
            generation | notification | extension | no) "no">
        extension (networking | facilitation | database | adaptation
            errorcorrect | retransmit | registration | security | no)
            "no"
```

```
            registration (home | visitor) "home"
            security (encryption | access) "access" >
<!ELEMENT rulemgt EMPTY >
<!ATTLIST rulemgt
        function (scripting | storing | interpreting) "scripting" >
<!ELEMENT automation EMPTY >
<- - method invocation, object specifier - ->
<!ATTLIST automation
        type (invocation | specifier) "invocation" >
```

This example shows two things. First, in the attribute list with specified values a "no" can be included. Second, a value can be further refined, such as registration in extension and then values of "home" and "visitor."

Declaring Element Type: Imagery

Here are some basic points one might get from brainstorming about the Imagery Facility:

■ Imagery activities
   ❑ Examining
   ❑ Processing
   ❑ Annotating
   ❑ Storing
   ❑ Displaying

```
<- - five activities - ->
<- - a vertical market facility - ->
<!ELEMENT imagery (examining, processing, annotating, storing,
displaying) >
<- - see ISO/IEC JTC SC24 WG1 Image Processing Interchange - ->
<!ELEMENT examining EMPTY >
<!ELEMENT processing EMPTY >
<!ELEMENT annotating EMPTY >
<!ELEMENT storing EMPTY >
<!ELEMENT displaying EMPTY >
```

This example is a "first draft" type since it only states five imaging activities without any attributes. You need more than this to be useful. Things that need to be considered are imagery applications and archives. Another important element is support applications that access imagery-related data. One also needs to consider image types, quality, annotations, and standards.

Part

Declaring Element Type: InfoSuper

Here are some basic points one might get from brainstorming about the Information Superhighways Facility:

- Think Internet functionality
- Six areas
  - ❏ Commerce
  - ❏ Resource discovery (search)
  - ❏ Intermediaries
  - ❏ Teleconferencing
  - ❏ Experimentation
  - ❏ User access
- Commercial concerns
  - ❏ Advertising
  - ❏ Monitoring
  - ❏ Costing
- Types of intermediaries
  - ❏ Broker
  - ❏ Intelligent agent
  - ❏ Mediator
  - ❏ Trader
- Types of teleconferencing
  - ❏ Collaboration
  - ❏ Mentoring
- User access issues
  - ❏ Interface level (novice or expert)
  - ❏ Profile management
  - ❏ Group association

```
<- - six potential facilities - ->
<- - a vertical market facility - ->
<- - search = resource discovery - ->
<- - access = user access - ->
<!ELEMENT InfoSuper (commerce, search, intermediaries, teleconferencing,
                     experimentation, access) >
```

```
<- - see ISO/IEC JTC SC24 WG1 Image Processing Interchange - ->
<!NOTATION ISA1 SYSTEM "http://www.myplace.com/comapp.exe" >
<!NOTATION ISA2 SYSTEM "http://www.myplace.com/search.exe" >
<!NOTATION ISA3 SYSTEM "http://www.myplace.com/annapp.exe" >
<!NOTATION ISA4 SYSTEM "http://www.myplace.com/storapp.exe" >
<!NOTATION ISA5 SYSTEM "http://www.myplace.com/display.exe" >
<!ELEMENT commerce EMPTY >
<ATTLIST commerce
        app notation (none | ISA1) "ISA1" >
<!ELEMENT search EMPTY >
<ATTLIST search
        app notation (none | ISA2) "ISA2" >
<!ELEMENT annotating EMPTY >
<ATTLIST annotating
        app notation (none | ISA3) "ISA3" >
<!ELEMENT storing  EMPTY >
<ATTLIST storing
        app notation (none | ISA4) "ISA4" >
<!ELEMENT displaying EMPTY >
<ATTLIST displaying
        app notation (none | ISA5) "ISA5" >
```

This theoretical example shows how one might call applications for processing. The ISA1 to ISA5 are arbitrary names representing InfoSuper application.

Declaring Element Type: Manufacturing

Here are some basic points one might get from brainstorming about the Manufacturing Facility:

- Three types of specialization
  - ❏ Policy variable management
  - ❏ History management
  - ❏ STEP standards
- Concerns of history management
  - ❏ Access
  - ❏ Controls

■ Issues for a product data service
  ❏ Engineering concurrency
  ❏ Technological integration
  ❏ Encapsulated object-oriented interface
  ❏ Fast large model execution (fine-grained object level)

```
<- - three identified types of specialization - ->
<- - a dozen plus potential types - ->
<- - see Standard Data Access Interface Specification - ->
<- - Part 22 ISO 10303-22, 1994 or updates - ->
<- - spec1 = policy variable management - ->
<- - spec2 = history management - ->
<- - spec3 = product data service - ->
<!ELEMENT Manufacturing (spec1, spec2, spec3) >
<- - manufacturing into our company may not be - ->
<- - introduced prior to 2005 - ->

<- - need to identify FUNCTIONS such as engineering, - ->
<- - process and quality controls, sales, finance, human resources - ->

<- - need to identify computational resource COMPONENTS - ->
<- - such as operating systems, databases, - ->
<- - equipment interfaces, hardware - ->

<- - for spec1 need to access business rules and policy variables - ->
<- - need processing applications - ->

<- - for spec2 need storage location, format and type - ->
<- - also need access application - ->
<- - identify objects as events; be able to display response - ->
<- - consider Event Facility - ->

<- - for spec3 need to integrate STEP standard - ->
```

In this example rather than concrete names such as policy, history, or product, abstract names were used to show how one can continue to add to an element if there are additions. For example, spec4 could be factory simulation which has been identified as a potential specialization.

This example is a placeholder for later enhancements. It does show how one can make comments in a DTD for further use.

Declaring Element Type: Simulation

Here are some basic points one might get from brainstorming about the Distributed Simulation Facility:

- Seven areas
  - ❏ Types
  - ❏ Simulation management
  - ❏ Time management
  - ❏ Aircraft and vehicle states
  - ❏ Flight data
  - ❏ Adaptation
  - ❏ Environment
- Categories of simulation
  - ❏ Air traffic control
  - ❏ War gaming
  - ❏ Video gaming
- Management issues
  - ❏ Configuring
  - ❏ Component control
    - ● Choosing
    - ● Specifying
    - ● Allocating
    - ● Instantiating
    - ● Start ensuring
    - ● Status monitoring
    - ● Shut-down
    - ● State checking
  - ❏ Identifying
- Basic component commands
  - ❏ Start
  - ❏ Pause
  - ❏ Resume
  - ❏ Stop

Part **III**

- Adaptation issues
  - ❑ Location of airways
  - ❑ Fixes
  - ❑ Airspace definitions
- Environmental types
  - ❑ Weather
  - ❑ Terrain

Because this facility requires highly specialized knowledge for industries such as the military, gaming design, aircraft traffic control, and weather prediction, it is not discussed further here.

Declaring Element Type: OAGI

Here are some basic points one might get from brainstorming about the Oil and Gas Industry Facility:

- Three concerns
  - ❑ Data (large amount)
  - ❑ Algorithms
  - ❑ Storage
- Specific industry definitions

Because this facility requires highly specialized knowledge for a particular industry, it is not discussed further here.

Declaring Element Type: Accounting

Here are some basic points one might get from brainstorming about the Accounting Facility:

- Specific functionality across industries
- Activities (electronic)
  - ❑ Money exchange
  - ❑ Payroll
  - ❑ Purchases
  - ❑ Sales
  - ❑ Online charges

```
<- - consider the incorporation of CORBAservices such as  - ->
<- - Life Cycle, Trader, Transaction, Security, Query, Licensing - ->

<- - from Financial Accounting Standards Board (FASB) see - ->
<- - Generally Accepted Accounting Principles (GAAP) - ->
<- - Generally Accepted Auditing Standards (GAAS) - ->

<- - consider using other facilities such as Information Superhighways,
- ->
<- - Distributed Simulation - - >

<- - consider its use by other facilities such as manufacturing - ->

<!ELEMENT accounting (receive, pay) >
<- - identify the local accounting infrastructure logically first - ->
<- - integrate the standards as possible - ->
```

This is also a placeholder. What is important is to use XML to assist in identifying the local accounting system logically. Most accounting systems are proprietary, but are built on GAAP, GAAS, and IRS requirements.

Declaring Element Type: AppDev

Here are some basic points one might get from brainstorming about the Application Development Facility:

■ Six areas
  ❏ Technical engineering
  ❏ Applications components for reuse
  ❏ Technical management (change and reuse)
  ❏ Project management
  ❏ Processing support
  ❏ Framework
■ Types of technical engineering
  ❏ System
  ❏ Software
  ❏ Process
■ Phases of project management
  ❏ Plan

- ❏ Estimate
- ❏ Risk analysis
- ❏ Tracking
- ■ Types of processing support
  - ❏ Text
  - ❏ Numerical
  - ❏ Figure
- ■ Concerns of framework
  - ❏ Object management
  - ❏ Process management
  - ❏ Communication
  - ❏ Operating system
  - ❏ User
  - ❏ Policy enforcement

```
<- - three identified types of specialization - ->
<- - a dozen-plus potential types - ->
<- - see Standard Data Access Interface Specification - ->
<- - Part 22 ISO 10303-22, 1994 or updates - ->
<- - if1 = system engineering interfaces - ->
<- - if2 = software engineering interfaces - ->
<- - if3 = life cycle process engineering interfaces - ->
<!ELEMENT AppDev (if1, if2, if3) >
<- - need to consider the location of data and type of processing - ->
<- - applications required for each interface - ->
<- - make this module by individual interface - ->
```

This is also a placeholder. This facility requires a large number of interfaces and tools. The tool types include technical engineering, technical management, project management, and support. Here is a "brief" list of interface types (number of identified interfaces for that type):

- ■ System engineering (9)
- ■ Software engineering (13)
- ■ Life cycle process engineering (4)
- ■ Technical management (5)
- ■ Project management (5)
- ■ Support (6)

- User communication (3)
- Environment administration (8)
- Framework (7)

Would you need to work with all 60 of these interfaces? The answer is probably no. Remember that this facility is a generic place for handling the selection, development, building, and evolution of the applications needed to support an informational systems strategy.

Declaring Element Type: Mapping

Here are some basic points one might get from brainstorming about the Mapping Facility:

- Two areas
  - ❏ Access
  - ❏ Display
- Needs to move from special use to everyday use

```
<- - generally bundled as data access, analysis, and display - ->
<- - analysis function should be under modeling and simulation - ->
<!ELEMENT mapping (access, display)
```

This is a placeholder. This facility is being specified by OGIS Ltd. The effort is known as the Open Geodata Interoperability Specification.

Final Thoughts, Summary, and Conclusions

This chapter is divided into three areas. Final thoughts are just ideas that have evolved out of doing this book. The summary relies on the basic principle of telling people what you are going to say (introduction), telling them in detail (the body of the book), and reminding them of what you said (final chapter). Conclusions are where one can go with this information and what actions or consequences result from the information in the book.

Final Thoughts

The Common Object Request Broker Architecture (CORBA) and the Extensible Markup Language (XML) are two very dynamic technologies for handling object-oriented data. Perhaps their evolutions can have a common path of friendship. It seems that:

- CORBA has to have further growth defining its CORBAfacilities and domains.
- XML has to grow to handle data in multiple locations and in multiple display formats.

It appears there is a potential for some kind of integration of CORBA and XML. An area that must be included is modeling and the place of the Interface Definition Language (IDL) in this "merging" of technologies.

Summary

The book began with a look at the practical implications of XML such as its grammar and benefits. There were also three comparisons given as XML to SGML, HTML, and Java.

The next discussion was concerned with the place and order of a production rule because of its importance in an implementing context. There was an overview of key XML concepts:

- Production rules overview
- Well-formed documents
- Valid documents
- Logical structures
- Physical structures
- XML processor constraints

Next there was a discussion of ten frequently asked questions about a DTD. The rest of the book is an outgrowth of the answers from this FAQ.

Then there was a look at the fundamental process for developing a document type definition (DTD). The ideas were extended in the chapters on developing DTDs for CORBAservices and CORBAfacilities. This look also included discussions on key tools for developing a DTD and XML documents—parsers, editors, and browsers.

The next topic covered was modeling. The focus was on the Document Object Model (DOM). It was shown how the DOM permits one to view an XML document as a data holder and as an object of the CORBA paradigm. It was stated that the DOM should be the API standard for handling XML documents in applications, browsers, and editors. Also included was a four-part example of Java code, an XML DTD, XML markup, and DOM output.

Three developing Web technologies and their implications for developing XML applications for CORBA were then discussed:

- Distributed Component Architecture Modeling (DCAM)
- Interface Definition Language (IDL)
- Unified Modeling Language (UML)

To close out model and definitional languages there was a discussion on the importance of Web Interface Definition Language (WIDL), a new Web technology for conceptually developing XML applications for CORBA from webMethods. It was stated that this technology goes hand-in-hand with the Document Object Model (DOM) and Distributed Component Architecture Modeling (DCAM) technologies.

The "headlines" metaphor was used to establish the fundamentals of CORBA. This was a "search" for the components, features, functions, or parts of CORBA that can be equated to XML elements, attributes, or entities. The search included a look at the architecture, the ORB, domains, CORBAservices, Security Service, and CORBAfacilities.

Next there was a brief review of the essentials of CORBAservices. This review established descriptive information for the development for XML examples using CORBAservices as a document type labeled *services* (Chapter 12).

Then there was a brief review of the essentials of CORBAfacilities. This review was used to establish descriptive information for the development of a document type definition (DTD) using CORBAfacilities as a document type labeled *facilities* (Chapter 14).

Next was a consideration of the ten general key design and development issues. Specific issues were also considered. These issues come in two categories, single environment or multiple environments. A single environment is considering CORBA itself. A multiple environment is considering CORBA and XML integration.

The next four chapters dealt with the design issues for developing XML DTDs for CORBA domains, CORBAservices, security as a CORBA service, and CORBAfacilities. The discussion on the DTD CORBA domains was at a very high level because of the level of development on domains. The discussion on a DTD for CORBAservices presented a model filled with potentials. The premise was that an XML document can handle data and that CORBA is fundamentally a series of interfaces, thus, one can design an XML document that organizes and declares the variables that might go into the interfaces. The discussion on DTD security as a service was a look at the potentials in the DTD for CORBAservices. The final discussion was on developing XML examples for CORBAfacilities. This discussion was basically a "what-if" one rather than a "how-to" chapter.

Conclusions

The major conclusion is that one needs to have experiences with both XML and CORBA to see where object-oriented technology may go. Both of these technologies are in stages of growth and potential.

If one wants to further the ideas given in this book, the place to begin is CORBAservices. If one is a vendor, one should consider in the design of a facility or a domain how XML might be used to enhance the interface or product.

This book acknowledges the first design goal of the XML Recommendation states "XML shall be straightforwardly usable over the Internet," but it has been demonstrated that XML has broad application in such as areas as e-commerce. Taking a broad sweep, this book focused on <u>XML design</u> using the structures of CORBA so one might get a new perspective on programming in an object-oriented environment.

This book does not teach XML, but discusses design for experienced object-oriented developers. One needs to comprehend how an analysis of an environment, CORBA, assists in design and development of XML elements, attributes, and entities that reflect that environment.

The potentials of CORBA and XML have not yet begun to be explored or exploited. The future is full of possibilities!

Part IV

Appendixes

Included in This Part:

- Appendix A—Terms and Definitions

- Appendix B—XML Alphabetical Production Rules List

- Appendix C—XML Production Rules

- Appendix D—Constraints

- Appendix E—XML Web Sites

- Appendix F—XML Markup Examples

Appendix A

Terms and Definitions

Note: When "Rule n" is referred to in this glossary, it is a reference to a production rule in XML Recommendation 1.0 (10 February 1998). Appendix C lists these production rules.[1]

Term	Definition
application	The software module on behalf of which an XML processor does its work.
attribute	Governed by Rule 41. Used to associate name-value pairs with elements.
attribute list	The specified or declared attributes within a tag.
attribute-list declaration	Governed by Rules 52-53. Specifies the name, data type, and default value (if any) of each attribute associated with a given element type.
attribute type	Governed by Rule 54. Three kinds: a string type, a set of tokenized types, and enumerated types.
CDATA section	Governed by Rules 18-21. May occur anywhere character data may occur. It is used to escape blocks of text containing characters that would otherwise be recognized as markup. It begins with the string "<![CDATA[" and ends with the string "]]>".
character	Governed by Rules 2 and 84-89. An atomic unit of text as specified by ISO/IEC 10646. Legal characters are tab, carriage return, line feed, and the legal graphic characters of Unicode and ISO/IEC 10646.

[1]   When "rule" is used in the definitions, it is a reference to a "production rule."

Term	Definition
character data	Governed by Rule 14. It is any text that is not markup.
character reference	Governed by Rule 66. A specific character in the ISO/IEC 10646 character set; for example, one not directly accessible from available input devices.
children	Governed by Rules 47-50. Elements without content.
class	Within XML, a class is a document type. Within the publishing world, examples are manuals, novels, and letters. Examples as used in this book are domains, services, and facilities.
comment	Governed by Rule 15. Marked off by <-- -->. May appear anywhere in a document outside other markup. It may appear within the document type declaration at places allowed by the grammar.
compatibility	A feature of XML included solely to ensure that XML remains compatible with SGML.
conditional section	Governed by Rules 61-65. Portion of the document type declaration external subset which is included in, or excluded from, the logical structure of the DTD based on the keyword which governs it.
constraint	A rule for an XML processor for determining declaration errors. A constraint can be either one of well-formedness or validity.
content	Governed by Rule 43. It usually is the text between an element's start-tag and end-tag. It can also be character data, entity references, CDATA sections, processing instructions, and comments.
content model	Describes what might occur with instances of a given element type. It is found in the DTD.
content of elements	Governed by Rule 43. The text between the start-tag and end-tag is called the element's content.
CORBAservices	Provides services for objects.
CORBAfacilities	Provides services for applications.
CORBA domains	Provides services for functions.
declaration	A formal statement for production. Rules that declare include document types, element types, attribute lists, entity, text, and notation.

Term	Definition
default declaration	Governed by Rule 60. Declares how an XML processor should react if a declared attribute is absent in a document.
delimited text	Text surrounded by a delimiter that is a special character that states the limits of a string. Common delimiters are quotation marks, single and double.
document	Not defined in the XML Recommendation. Since XML is a subset of SGML, one might use the definition in ISO 8879. A document can be "a collection of information that is processed as a unit." A document can be located in more than one physical location or unit.
document element	See root element.
document entity	Governed by Rule 1. Serves as the starting point for the XML processor and may contain the whole document.
document type	A document class with a common set of properties. See class.
document type declaration	Defines constraints on the logical structure and to support the use of predefined storage units and must appear before the first element in the document.
document type definition	(DTD) The grammar for a class of documents found in the XML document type declaration that contains or points to markup declarations.
EBNF	Extended Backus-Naur Form of notation. The notation to form the production rules that uses as its basic form the right-handed form of symbol ::= expression. This reads that a symbol consists of an expression. The expression can have multiple parts.
element	Governed by Rule 39. Content of a document delimited by start-tags and end-tags or, for empty elements, by an empty-element tag. A logical unit within an XML document.
element type declaration	Governed by Rule 45. Constrains the element's content.
empty-element tag	Governed by Rule 44. A logical structure delimiter. May be used for any element that has no content.

Term	Definition
encoding declaration	Governed by Rule 78. Parsed entities stored in an encoding other than UTF-8 or UTF-16 must begin with a text declaration containing an encoding declaration. It is part of the XML declaration.
end-tag	Governed by Rule 42. It is the end of every non-empty XML element. It echoes the element's type as given in the start-tag.
entity	Any data that can be treated as a "virtual" storage unit.
entity declaration	Governed by Rules 70-74. The Name identifies the entity in an entity reference or, in the case of an unparsed entity, in the value of an ENTITY or ENTITIES attribute.
entity reference	Governed by Rule 67. The content of a named entity. It signifies that a copy of the entity is to be included at this point.
entity value	Governed by Rule 9. It is the literal text within an internal entity declaration.
enumerated attributes type	Governed by Rule 57. There are two kinds of enumerated types: notation and enumeration.
error	A violation of the rules of the Working Recommendation. The results are undefined. A conforming processor may detect and report an error and may recover from it.
Extended Backus-Naur Form	See EBNF.
Extensible Markup Language	(XML) Describes a class of data objects called XML documents and partially describes the behavior of computer programs which process them. XML is an application profile or restricted form of SGML, the Standard Generalized Markup Language (ISO 8879). By construction, XML documents conform to SGML documents.
external entity	Governed by Rule 75. Any entity not an internal entity.

Term	Definition
external subset	Governed by Rule 30. Consists of a series of complete markup declarations of the types allowed by the non-terminal symbol markupdecl, interspersed with white space or parameter-entity references.
fatal error	An error which a conforming XML processor must detect and report to the application. Once a fatal error is detected, however, the processor must not continue normal processing (that is, it must not continue to pass character data and information about the document's logical structure to the application in the normal way).
generic identifier	The name assigned to an element type. The "name" of a tag <GI> </GI>.
general entities	Entities for use within the document content.
grammar (XML)	The rules for creating markup that are defined by a document type definition (DTD) and the parsing constraints of the XML Recommendation.
IANA	(Internet Assigned Numbers Authority) "Official Names for Character Sets," ed. Keld Simonsen et al. See ftp://ftp.isi.edu/in-notes/iana/assignments/character-sets.
IETF RFC 1766	(Internet Engineering Task Force). RFC 1766: "Tags for the Identification of Languages," ed. H. Alvestrand. 1995.
internal entity	An entity whose value is given in its entity declaration in the DTD. An internal entity is a parsed entity. For example, <!ENTITY QoS "Quality of Service">.
interoperability	A non-binding recommendation to increase the chances that XML documents can be processed by the existing installed base of SGML processors which predate the Web SGML Adaptations Annex to ISO 8879.
ISO	Refers to the International Organization for Standardization (English) or Organisation Internationale de Normalisation (French). It is not an acronym.

Term	Definition
ISO 639	(International Organization for Standardization). ISO 639:1988 (E). Code for the representation of names of languages. [Geneva]: International Organization for Standardization, 1988.
ISO 3166	(International Organization for Standardization). ISO 3166-1:1997 (E). Codes for the representation of names of countries and their subdivisions—Part 1: Country codes [Geneva]: International Organization for Standardization, 1997.
ISO/IEC 10646	(International Organization for Standardization). ISO/IEC 10646-1993 (E). Information technology—Universal Multiple-Octet Coded Character Set (UCS)—Part 1: Architecture and Basic Multilingual Plane. [Geneva]: International Organization for Standardization, 1993 (plus amendments AM 1 through AM 7).
language identification	Governed by Rules 33-38. Identifies the natural or formal language in which the content is written. The language identifiers as defined by IETF RFC 1766, "Tags for the Identification of Languages."
letter	Consists of an alphabetic or syllabic base character possibly followed by one or more combining characters, or of an ideographic character.
literal	Any quoted string not containing the quotation mark used as a delimiter for that string. Literals are used for specifying the content of internal entities (EntityValue, Rule 9), the values of attributes (AttValue, Rule 10), and external identifiers (SystemLiteral, Rule 11).
logical structure	The document structure that is declarations, elements, comments, character references, and processing instructions, all of which are indicated in the document by explicit markup.
markup	The tags that describe the document's storage layout and logical structure: start-tags, end-tags, empty-element tags, entity references, character references, comments, CDATA section delimiters, document type declarations, and processing instructions.

Term	Definition
markup declaration	Either an element type declaration, an attribute-list declaration, an entity declaration, or a notation declaration.
match (of strings or names)	Two strings or names being compared must be identical. Characters with multiple possible representations in ISO/IEC 10646 match only if they have the same representation in both strings.
mixed content	Governed by Rule 51. Mixed content is when elements of an element type may contain character data, optionally interspersed with child elements.
name	Governed by Rules 5-8. A token beginning with a letter or one of a few punctuation characters, and continuing with letters, digits, hyphens, underscores, colons, or full stops, together known as name characters.
namespace	A set of unique names. The colon (:) may be used to resolve the issue when a document uses two DTDs that both use an element type or entity with the same name. For example, the namespaces would be DTDname1:samename and DTDname2:samename.
nesting	A property of well-formed documents, that is, the logical instances are contained correctly within each other.
Nmtoken	(name token) Any mixture of name characters.
non-validating parser	A parser that checks the well-formedness constraints.
notation declaration	Governed by Rule 82. Identifies by name the format of unparsed entities, the format of elements that bear a notation attribute, or the application to which a processing instruction is addressed. For example, the format could be BMP image.
parameter entities	Entities for use within the DTD.
parsed data	Data that has to be parsed are made up of characters, either character or markup.
parsed entity	Contains text, a sequence of characters, which may represent markup or character data. Invoked by name using entity references.

IV

Part

Term	Definition
parser	A process that analyzes notated text and determines if a notation is correct in accordance with defined grammar. An XML parser analyzes markup and content and uses well-formedness constraints and perhaps validity constraints.
physical structure	The document structure that is units or entities. A document begins in a "root" or document entity.
processing instruction	(PI) Governed by Rule 16. Allows documents to contain instructions for applications.
processor	A software module that reads XML documents and provides access to their content and structure. It reads XML data and the information and provides the results to an application.
production rule	See Appendix B for a listing of XML production rules. Uses the EBNF notation of symbol ::= expression.
prolog	The part of the XML document (Rule 1) that includes the XML declaration and DTD. It precedes the actual document element.
replacement text	A parsed entity's contents and this text are considered an integral part of the document.
reserved names	Any name beginning with the string "xml", or any string which would match (('X'|'x') ('M'|'m') ('L'|'l')).
root element	The element that contains all the other elements. The root element is specified in the document type declaration. It is the point where the parser begins processing.
standalone document declaration	Governed by Rule 32. May appear as a component of the XML declaration. Signals whether or not there are such declarations which appear external to the document entity.
start-tag	Governed by Rule 40. The beginning of every non-empty XML element.
string	A sequence of characters usually delimited by quotation marks, single or double.
style sheet	An instruction set that specifies how each structural object within an XML document is to be formatted.

Term	Definition
tag	A type of markup that is delimited by a less-than symbol or right-handed bracket and the greater-than symbol or left-handed bracket. Usually refers to the start-tag and end-tag of an element.
text	Consists of intermingled character data and markup.
text declaration	Governed by Rule 77. External parsed entities may each begin with a text declaration. The text declaration must be provided literally, not by reference to a parsed entity. No text declaration may appear at any position other than the beginning of an external parsed entity.
textual object	It is a well-formed XML document if: it matches the production labeled document, meets all the XML Specification's well-formedness constraints, and each of the referenced parsed entities is well-formed.
token	A document indivisible unit type. Examples as used in markup are DOCTYPE, ELEMENT, and ATTLIST.
Unicode	The Unicode Consortium. *The Unicode Standard, Version 2.0*. Reading, Mass.: Addison-Wesley Developers Press, 1996.
unparsed entities	Invoked by name, given in the value of ENTITY or ENTITIES attributes.
valid document	An XML document that follows all the rules specified by its document type declaration.
validating parser	A parser that checks for the constraints as defined in the XML Recommendation.
validity constraint	A rule that applies to all valid XML documents. Violations of validity constraints are errors; they must, at user option, be reported by validating XML processors.
well-formed document	An XML document that conforms to the XML Recommendation but does not necessarily adhere to the validity constraints. A textual object is a well-formed XML document if: ■ Taken as a whole, it matches the production labeled document.

Term	Definition
well-formed document	(cont.)
	■ It meets all the well-formedness constraints given in this specification.
	■ Each of the parsed entities referenced directly or indirectly within the document is well-formed.
well-formedness constraint	A rule which applies to all well-formed XML documents. Violations of well-formedness constraints are fatal errors.
white space	Governed by Rule 3. Consists of one or more space (#x20) characters, carriage returns, line feeds, or tabs.

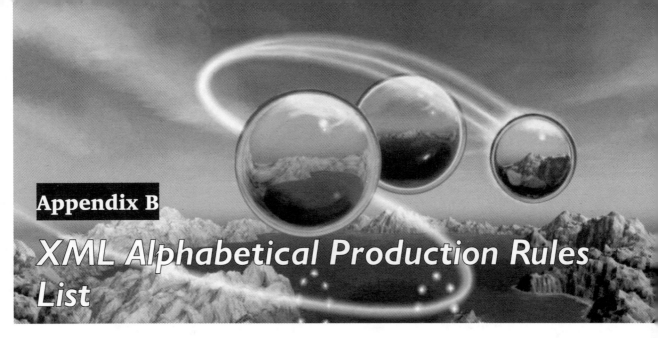

Appendix B
XML Alphabetical Production Rules List

The number following each production rule refers to its number. Please see Appendix C.

Appendix C

XML Production Rules

Note: These rules are from Extensible Markup Language 1.0 W3C
Recommendation (10 February 1998).

```
[1] document ::= prolog element Misc*


[2] Char ::= #x9 | #xA | #xD | [#x20-#xD7FF] |
    [#xE000-#xFFFD] | [#x10000-#x10FFFF]/* any Unicode
    character, excluding the surrogate blocks, FFFE, and
    FFFF. */


[3] S ::= (#x20 | #x9 | #xD | #xA)+


[4] NameChar ::= Letter | Digit | '.' | '-' | '_' | ':' |
    CombiningChar | Extender
[5] Name ::= (Letter | '_' | ':') (NameChar)*
[6] Names ::= Name (S Name)*
[7] Nmtoken ::= (NameChar)+
[8] Nmtokens ::= Nmtoken (S Nmtoken)*


[9] EntityValue ::= '"' ([^%&"] | PEReference | Reference)* '"'
    | "'" ([^%&'] | PEReference | Reference)* "'"
[10] AttValue ::= '"' ([^<&"] | Reference)* '"'
    | "'" ([^<&'] | Reference)* "'"
[11] SystemLiteral ::= ('"' [^"]* '"') | ("'" [^']* "'")
```

```
[12] PubidLiteral ::= '"' PubidChar* '"' | "'" (PubidChar
     - "'")* "'"
[13] PubidChar ::= #x20 | #xD | #xA | [a-zA-Z0-9] |
     [-'()+,./:=?;!*#@$_%]
```

```
[14] CharData ::= [^<&]* - ([^<&]* ']]>' [^<&]*)
```

```
[15] Comment ::= '<!--' ((Char - '-') | ('-' (Char -
     '-')))* '-->'
```

```
[16] PI ::= '<?' PITarget (S (Char* - (Char* '?>'
     Char*)))? '?>'
[17] PITarget ::= Name - (('X' | 'x') ('M' | 'm') ('L' |
     'l'))
```

```
[18] CDSect ::= CDStart CData CDEnd
[19] CDStart ::= '<![CDATA['
[20] CData ::= (Char* - (Char* ']]>' Char*))
[21] CDEnd ::= ']]>'
```

```
[22] prolog ::= XMLDecl? Misc* (doctypedecl Misc*)?
[23] XMLDecl ::= '<?xml' VersionInfo EncodingDecl?
     SDDecl? S? '?>'
[24] VersionInfo ::= S 'version' Eq (' VersionNum ' | "
     VersionNum ")
[25] Eq ::= S? '=' S?
[26] VersionNum ::= ([a-zA-Z0-9_.:] | '-')+
[27] Misc ::= Comment | PI | S
```

Warning: [24] implies that one can state version=1.0. This is incorrect; it has to be either version='1.0' or version="1.0". The quotation marks are literals. [24] should read VersionInfo ::= S 'version' Eq (""VersionNum"" | "" VersionNum "").

```
[28] doctypedecl ::= '<!DOCTYPE' S Name (S ExternalID)?
     S? ('[' (markupdecl | PEReference | S)* ']' S?)? '>'[
     VC: Root Element Type ]
[29] markupdecl ::= elementdecl | AttlistDecl |
     EntityDecl | NotationDecl | PI | Comment [ VC: Proper
     Declaration/PE Nesting ]
     [ WFC: PEs in Internal Subset ]


[30] extSubset ::= TextDecl? extSubsetDecl
[31] extSubsetDecl ::= ( markupdecl | conditionalSect |
     PEReference | S )*


[32] SDDecl ::= S 'standalone' Eq (("'" ('yes' | 'no')
     "'") | ('"' ('yes' | 'no') '"')) [ VC: Standalone
     Document Declaration ]


[33] LanguageID ::= Langcode ('-' Subcode)*
[34] Langcode ::= ISO639Code | IanaCode | UserCode
[35] ISO639Code ::= ([a-z] | [A-Z]) ([a-z] | [A-Z])
[36] IanaCode ::= ('i' | 'I') '-' ([a-z] | [A-Z])+
[37] UserCode ::= ('x' | 'X') '-' ([a-z] | [A-Z])+
[38] Subcode ::= ([a-z] | [A-Z])+


[39] element ::= EmptyElemTag
     | STag content ETag[ WFC: Element Type Match ]
     [ VC: Element Valid ]


[40] STag ::= '<' Name (S Attribute)* S? '>'[ WFC: Unique
     Att Spec ]
[41] Attribute ::= Name Eq AttValue[ VC: Attribute Value
     Type ]
     [ WFC: No External Entity References ]
     [ WFC: No < in Attribute Values ]
```

[42] ETag ::= '</' Name S? '>'

[43] content ::= (element | CharData | Reference | CDSect
        | PI | Comment)*

[44] EmptyElemTag ::= '<' Name (S Attribute)* S? '/>'[
        WFC: Unique Att Spec]

[45] elementdecl ::= '<!ELEMENT' S Name S contentspec S?
        '>'[VC: Unique Element Type Declaration]
[46] contentspec ::= 'EMPTY' | 'ANY' | Mixed | children

[47] children ::= (choice | seq) ('?' | '*' | '+')?
[48] cp ::= (Name | choice | seq) ('?' | '*' | '+')?
[49] choice ::= '(' S? cp (S? '|' S? cp)* S? ')'[VC:
        Proper Group/PE Nesting]
[50] seq ::= '(' S? cp (S? ',' S? cp)* S? ')'[VC:
        Proper Group/PE Nesting]

[51] Mixed ::= '(' S? '#PCDATA' (S? '|' S? Name)* S? ')*'

        | '(' S? '#PCDATA' S? ')' [VC: Proper Group/PE Nesting]
        [VC: No Duplicate Types]

[52] AttlistDecl ::= '<!ATTLIST' S Name AttDef* S? '>'

[53] AttDef ::= S Name S AttType S DefaultDecl

[54] AttType ::= StringType | TokenizedType |
        EnumeratedType
[55] StringType ::= 'CDATA'

```
[56] TokenizedType ::= 'ID'[ VC: ID ]
        [ VC: One ID per Element Type ]
        [ VC: ID Attribute Default ]
        | 'IDREF'[ VC: IDREF ]
        | 'IDREFS'[ VC: IDREF ]
        | 'ENTITY'[ VC: Entity Name ]
        | 'ENTITIES'[ VC: Entity Name ]
        | 'NMTOKEN'[ VC: Name Token ]
        | 'NMTOKENS'[ VC: Name Token ]


[57] EnumeratedType ::= NotationType | Enumeration
[58] NotationType ::= 'NOTATION' S '(' S? Name (S? '|' S?
        Name)* S? ')' [ VC: Notation Attributes ]
[59] Enumeration ::= '(' S? Nmtoken (S? '|' S? Nmtoken)*
        S? ')'[ VC: Enumeration ]


[60] DefaultDecl ::= '#REQUIRED' | '#IMPLIED'
        | (('#FIXED' S)? AttValue)[ VC: Required Attribute ]
        [ VC: Attribute Default Legal ]
        [ WFC: No < in Attribute Values ]
        [ VC: Fixed Attribute Default ]


[61] conditionalSect ::= includeSect | ignoreSect
[62] includeSect ::= '<![' S? 'INCLUDE' S? '['
        extSubsetDecl ']]>'
[63] ignoreSect ::= '<![' S? 'IGNORE' S? '['
        ignoreSectContents* ']]>'
[64] ignoreSectContents ::= Ignore ('<!['
        ignoreSectContents ']]>' Ignore)*
[65] Ignore ::= Char* - (Char* ('<![' | ']]>') Char*)


[66] CharRef ::= '&#' [0-9]+ ';'
        | '&#x' [0-9a-fA-F]+ ';'[ WFC: Legal Character ]
```

[67] Reference ::= EntityRef | CharRef
[68] EntityRef ::= '&' Name ';'[WFC: Entity Declared]
        [VC: Entity Declared]
        [WFC: Parsed Entity]
        [WFC: No Recursion]
[69] PEReference ::= '%' Name ';'[VC: Entity Declared]
        [WFC: No Recursion]
        [WFC: In DTD]

[70] EntityDecl ::= GEDecl | PEDecl
[71] GEDecl ::= '<!ENTITY' S Name S EntityDef S? '>'
[72] PEDecl ::= '<!ENTITY' S '%' S Name S PEDef S? '>'
[73] EntityDef ::= EntityValue | (ExternalID NDataDecl?)
[74] PEDef ::= EntityValue | ExternalID

[75] ExternalID ::= 'SYSTEM' S SystemLiteral
        | 'PUBLIC' S PubidLiteral S SystemLiteral
[76] NDataDecl ::= S 'NDATA' S Name[VC: Notation
        Declared]

[77] TextDecl ::= '<?xml' VersionInfo? EncodingDecl S?
        '?>'

[78] extParsedEnt ::= TextDecl? content
[79] extPE ::= TextDecl? extSubsetDecl

[80] EncodingDecl ::= S 'encoding' Eq ('"' EncName '"' |
        "'" EncName "'")
[81] EncName ::= [A-Za-z] ([A-Za-z0-9._] | '-')*/*
        Encoding name contains only Latin characters */

[82] NotationDecl ::= '<!NOTATION' S Name S (ExternalID |
        PublicID) S? '>'
[83] PublicID ::= 'PUBLIC' S PubidLiteral

```
[84] Letter ::= BaseChar | Ideographic
[85] BaseChar ::= [#x0041-#x005A] | [#x0061-#x007A] |
        [#x00C0-#x00D6] | [#x00D8-#x00F6] | [#x00F8-#x00FF] |
        [#x0100-#x0131] | [#x0134-#x013E] | [#x0141-#x0148] |
        [#x014A-#x017E] | [#x0180-#x01C3] | [#x01CD-#x01F0] |
        [#x01F4-#x01F5] | [#x01FA-#x0217] | [#x0250-#x02A8] |
        [#x02BB-#x02C1] | #x0386 | [#x0388-#x038A] | #x038C |
        [#x038E-#x03A1] | [#x03A3-#x03CE] | [#x03D0-#x03D6] |
        #x03DA | #x03DC | #x03DE | #x03E0 | [#x03E2-#x03F3] |
        [#x0401-#x040C] | [#x040E-#x044F] | [#x0451-#x045C] |
        [#x045E-#x0481] | [#x0490-#x04C4] | [#x04C7-#x04C8] |
        [#x04CB-#x04CC] | [#x04D0-#x04EB] | [#x04EE-#x04F5] |
        [#x04F8-#x04F9] | [#x0531-#x0556] | #x0559 |
        [#x0561-#x0586] | [#x05D0-#x05EA] | [#x05F0-#x05F2] |
        [#x0621-#x063A] | [#x0641-#x064A] | [#x0671-#x06B7] |
        [#x06BA-#x06BE] | [#x06C0-#x06CE] | [#x06D0-#x06D3] |
        #x06D5 | [#x06E5-#x06E6] | [#x0905-#x0939] | #x093D |
        [#x0958-#x0961] | [#x0985-#x098C] | [#x098F-#x0990] |
        [#x0993-#x09A8] | [#x09AA-#x09B0] | #x09B2 |
        [#x09B6-#x09B9] | [#x09DC-#x09DD] | [#x09DF-#x09E1] |
        [#x09F0-#x09F1] | [#x0A05-#x0A0A] | [#x0A0F-#x0A10] |
        [#x0A13-#x0A28] | [#x0A2A-#x0A30] | [#x0A32-#x0A33] |
        [#x0A35-#x0A36] | [#x0A38-#x0A39] | [#x0A59-#x0A5C] |
        #x0A5E | [#x0A72-#x0A74] | [#x0A85-#x0A8B] | #x0A8D |
        [#x0A8F-#x0A91] | [#x0A93-#x0AA8] | [#x0AAA-#x0AB0] |
        [#x0AB2-#x0AB3] | [#x0AB5-#x0AB9] | #x0ABD | #x0AE0 |
        [#x0B05-#x0B0C] | [#x0B0F-#x0B10] | [#x0B13-#x0B28] |
        [#x0B2A-#x0B30] | [#x0B32-#x0B33] | [#x0B36-#x0B39] |
        #x0B3D | [#x0B5C-#x0B5D] | [#x0B5F-#x0B61] |
        [#x0B85-#x0B8A] | [#x0B8E-#x0B90] | [#x0B92-#x0B95] |
        [#x0B99-#x0B9A] | #x0B9C | [#x0B9E-#x0B9F] |
        [#x0BA3-#x0BA4] | [#x0BA8-#x0BAA] | [#x0BAE-#x0BB5] |
        [#x0BB7-#x0BB9] | [#x0C05-#x0C0C] | [#x0C0E-#x0C10] |
        [#x0C12-#x0C28] | [#x0C2A-#x0C33] | [#x0C35-#x0C39] |
        [#x0C60-#x0C61] | [#x0C85-#x0C8C] | [#x0C8E-#x0C90] |
        [#x0C92-#x0CA8] | [#x0CAA-#x0CB3] | [#x0CB5-#x0CB9] |
        #x0CDE | [#x0CE0-#x0CE1] | [#x0D05-#x0D0C] |
        [#x0D0E-#x0D10] | [#x0D12-#x0D28] | [#x0D2A-#x0D39] |
        [#x0D60-#x0D61] | [#x0E01-#x0E2E] | #x0E30 |
        [#x0E32-#x0E33] | [#x0E40-#x0E45] | [#x0E81-#x0E82] |
        #x0E84 | [#x0E87-#x0E88] | #x0E8A | #x0E8D |
        [#x0E94-#x0E97] | [#x0E99-#x0E9F] | [#x0EA1-#x0EA3] |
        #x0EA5 | #x0EA7 | [#x0EAA-#x0EAB] | [#x0EAD-#x0EAE] |
```

```
            #x0EB0 | [#x0EB2-#x0EB3] | #x0EBD | [#x0EC0-#x0EC4] |
            [#x0F40-#x0F47] | [#x0F49-#x0F69] | [#x10A0-#x10C5] |
            [#x10D0-#x10F6] | #x1100 | [#x1102-#x1103] |
            [#x1105-#x1107] | #x1109 | [#x110B-#x110C] |
            [#x110E-#x1112] | #x113C | #x113E | #x1140 | #x114C |
            #x114E | #x1150 | [#x1154-#x1155] | #x1159 |
            [#x115F-#x1161] | #x1163 | #x1165 | #x1167 | #x1169 |
            [#x116D-#x116E] | [#x1172-#x1173] | #x1175 | #x119E |
            #x11A8 | #x11AB | [#x11AE-#x11AF] | [#x11B7-#x11B8] |
            #x11BA | [#x11BC-#x11C2] | #x11EB | #x11F0 | #x11F9 |
            [#x1E00-#x1E9B] | [#x1EA0-#x1EF9] | [#x1F00-#x1F15] |
            [#x1F18-#x1F1D] | [#x1F20-#x1F45] | [#x1F48-#x1F4D] |
            [#x1F50-#x1F57] | #x1F59 | #x1F5B | #x1F5D |
            [#x1F5F-#x1F7D] | [#x1F80-#x1FB4] | [#x1FB6-#x1FBC] |
            #x1FBE | [#x1FC2-#x1FC4] | [#x1FC6-#x1FCC] |
            [#x1FD0-#x1FD3] | [#x1FD6-#x1FDB] | [#x1FE0-#x1FEC] |
            [#x1FF2-#x1FF4] | [#x1FF6-#x1FFC] | #x2126 |
            [#x212A-#x212B] | #x212E | [#x2180-#x2182] |
            [#x3041-#x3094] | [#x30A1-#x30FA] | [#x3105-#x312C] |
            [#xAC00-#xD7A3]
[86] Ideographic ::= [#x4E00-#x9FA5] | #x3007 |
            [#x3021-#x3029]
[87] CombiningChar ::= [#x0300-#x0345] | [#x0360-#x0361]
            | [#x0483-#x0486] | [#x0591-#x05A1] | [#x05A3-#x05B9] |
            [#x05BB-#x05BD] | #x05BF | [#x05C1-#x05C2] | #x05C4 |
            [#x064B-#x0652] | #x0670 | [#x06D6-#x06DC] |
            [#x06DD-#x06DF] | [#x06E0-#x06E4] | [#x06E7-#x06E8] |
            [#x06EA-#x06ED] | [#x0901-#x0903] | #x093C |
            [#x093E-#x094C] | #x094D | [#x0951-#x0954] |
            [#x0962-#x0963] | [#x0981-#x0983] | #x09BC | #x09BE |
            #x09BF | [#x09C0-#x09C4] | [#x09C7-#x09C8] |
            [#x09CB-#x09CD] | #x09D7 | [#x09E2-#x09E3] | #x0A02 |
            #x0A3C | #x0A3E | #x0A3F | [#x0A40-#x0A42] |
            [#x0A47-#x0A48] | [#x0A4B-#x0A4D] | [#x0A70-#x0A71] |
            [#x0A81-#x0A83] | #x0ABC | [#x0ABE-#x0AC5] |
            [#x0AC7-#x0AC9] | [#x0ACB-#x0ACD] | [#x0B01-#x0B03] |
            #x0B3C | [#x0B3E-#x0B43] | [#x0B47-#x0B48] |
            [#x0B4B-#x0B4D] | [#x0B56-#x0B57] | [#x0B82-#x0B83] |
            [#x0BBE-#x0BC2] | [#x0BC6-#x0BC8] | [#x0BCA-#x0BCD] |
            #x0BD7 | [#x0C01-#x0C03] | [#x0C3E-#x0C44] |
            [#x0C46-#x0C48] | [#x0C4A-#x0C4D] | [#x0C55-#x0C56] |
            [#x0C82-#x0C83] | [#x0CBE-#x0CC4] | [#x0CC6-#x0CC8] |
            [#x0CCA-#x0CCD] | [#x0CD5-#x0CD6] | [#x0D02-#x0D03] |
```

```
              [#x0D3E-#x0D43]  |  [#x0D46-#x0D48]  |  [#x0D4A-#x0D4D]  |
              #x0D57  |  #x0E31  |  [#x0E34-#x0E3A]  |  [#x0E47-#x0E4E]  |
              #x0EB1  |  [#x0EB4-#x0EB9]  |  [#x0EBB-#x0EBC]  |
              [#x0EC8-#x0ECD]  |  [#x0F18-#x0F19]  |  #x0F35   #x0F37  |
              #x0F39  |  #x0F3E  |  #x0F3F  |  [#x0F71-#x0F84]  |
              [#x0F86-#x0F8B]  |  [#x0F90-#x0F95]  |  #x0F97  |
              [#x0F99-#x0FAD]  |  [#x0FB1-#x0FB7]  |  #x0FB9  |
              [#x20D0-#x20DC]  |  #x20E1  |  [#x302A-#x302F]  |  #x3099  |
              #x309A
[88]  Digit ::=  [#x0030-#x0039]  |  [#x0660-#x0669]  |
              [#x06F0-#x06F9]  |  [#x0966-#x096F]  |  [#x09E6-#x09EF]  |
              [#x0A66-#x0A6F]  |  [#x0AE6-#x0AEF]  |  [#x0B66-#x0B6F]  |
              [#x0BE7-#x0BEF]  |  [#x0C66-#x0C6F]  |  [#x0CE6-#x0CEF]  |
              [#x0D66-#x0D6F]  |  [#x0E50-#x0E59]  |  [#x0ED0-#x0ED9]  |
              [#x0F20-#x0F29]
[89]  Extender ::=  #x00B7  |  #x02D0  |  #x02D1  |  #x0387  |
              #x0640  |  #x0E46  |  #x0EC6  |  #x3005  |  [#x3031-#x3035]  |
              [#x309D-#x309E]  |  [#x30FC-#x30FE]
```

IV

Part

Appendix D

Constraints

There are two types of constraints: well-formedness and validity. They are consequences for not following the production rules that are used to check for XML encoding errors by a conforming XML processor. This is a processor that follows or adheres or conforms to the well-formedness constraints in the Extensible Markup Language (XML) 1.0 W3 Recommendation (10 February 1998).

A well-formedness constraint is a rule that when not adhered to produces a fatal error and a conforming XML processor <u>must</u> report to the application. The processor terminates and gives a message. The processor cannot continue to pass character data and information about the document's logical structure to the application in the normal way.

A validity constraint is rule that when not adhered to produces an error where the results are unpredictable. A conforming processor may detect and report an error and may recover from it. Validating XML processors <u>must</u> report the errors at user option.

The constraints are grouped by subject. Any production rule that applies is given at the end of each constraint.

Note: For ease of readability, what is given below in many cases is synopses of the rules.

Well-Formedness Constraints

Element Type Match

The Name in an element's end-tag <u>must</u> match the element type in the start-tag. (Rule 39)

Entity Declared

In a document without a DTD, a document with only an internal DTD subset which contains no parameter entity references, or a document with "standalone='yes'", the Name given in the entity reference <u>must</u> match that in an entity declaration. Exception: Well-formed documents need not declare: amp, lt, gt, apos, or quot. (Rule 68)

In DTD

Parameter-entity references may only appear in the DTD. (Rule 69)

Legal Character

Characters referred to using character references <u>must</u> match the production for Char (Rule 2). If the character reference begins with "&#x", the digits and letters up to the terminating *;* provide a hexadecimal representation of the character's code point in ISO/IEC 10646. If it begins just with "&#", the digits up to the terminating *;* provide a decimal representation. (Rule 66)

No External Entity References

An attribute value cannot contain entity references to external entities. (Rule 41)

No Recursion

A parsed entity <u>must</u> not contain a recursive reference to itself, either directly or indirectly. (Rule 69)

No < in Attribute Values

The replacement text of a referenced entity in an attribute value (other than "<") <u>must</u> not contain a <. (Rules 41 and 60)

Parsed Entity

An entity reference <u>must</u> not contain the name of an unparsed entity. Unparsed entities may be referred to only in attribute values declared to be of type ENTITY or ENTITIES. (Rule 68)

PEs in Internal Subset

Parameter-entity references <u>must</u> be outside markup declarations. (This does not apply to references that occur in external parameter entities or to the external subset.) (Rule 29)

Unique Att Spec

An attribute name can appear <u>once</u> in the same start-tag or empty-element tag. (Rules 40 and 44)

Validity Constraints

Attribute Default Legal

The declared default value <u>must</u> meet the lexical constraints of the declared attribute type (Rules 54 and 60)

Attribute Value Type

The attribute <u>must</u> have been declared. The value <u>must</u> be of the type declared for it. (Rule 41)

Element Valid

An element is valid if there is a declaration matching *elementdecl* where the Name matches the element type, and one of the following holds:

■ The declaration matches EMPTY and the element has no content.

■ The declaration matches children (Rule 47) and the child element sequence belongs to the content model language, with optional white space (Rule 3) between each child element.

■ The declaration matches MIXED (Rule 51)and the content consists of character data (Rule 14) and child elements whose types match names in the content model.

IV

Part

■ The declaration matches ANY, and the types of any child elements have been declared. (Rule 39)

Entity Declared

In a document with an external subset or external parameter entities with "standalone='no'", the Name given in the entity reference <u>must</u> match that in an entity declaration. For interoperability, valid documents should declare the entities amp, lt, gt, apos, and quot in the form specified in "4.6 Predefined Entities" of the Recommendation. (Rules 68 and 69)

Entity Name

Values of types ENTITY and ENTITIES <u>must</u> match the Name and Names production (Rules 5 and 6) respectively. Each Name <u>must</u> match the name of an unparsed entity declared in the DTD. (Rule 56)

Enumeration

Values of this type <u>must</u> match one of the Nmtoken tokens in the declaration. For interoperability, the same Nmtoken should not occur more than once in the enumerated attribute types of a single element type. (Rule 59)

Fixed Attribute Default

When the default is #FIXED, the instances of that attribute <u>must</u> match the default value. (Rule 60)

ID

Values of type ID <u>must</u> match the Name production (Rule 5). ID values <u>must</u> uniquely identify the elements that bear them. (Rule 56)

One ID per Element Type

An element type <u>must</u> have only one ID attribute specified. (Rule 56)

ID Attribute Default

An ID attribute <u>must</u> have a declared default of #IMPLIED or #REQUIRED. (Rule 56)

IDREF

Values of types IDREF and IDREFS <u>must</u> match the Name and Names production (Rules 5 and 6) respectively. IDEF values <u>must</u> match the value of some ID attributes. (Rule 56)

Name Token

Values of types NMTOKEN and NMTOKENS <u>must</u> match the Nmtoken and NmTokens production. (Rules 7, 8, and 56)

No Duplicate Types

The same name <u>must</u> not appear more than once in a single mixed-content declaration. (Rule 51)

Notation Attributes

Values of this type <u>must</u> match one of the notation names included in the declaration; all notation names in the declaration <u>must</u> be declared. (Rule 58)

Notation Declared

The Name <u>must</u> match the declared name of a notation (Rule 82).

The *SystemLiteral* is called the entity's system identifier. The *PubidLiteral* is an external identifier, public. (Rule 76)

Proper Declaration/PE Nesting

Parameter-entity replacement text <u>must</u> be properly nested with markup declarations. If either the first character or the last character of a markup declaration is contained in the replacement text for a parameter-entity reference, both <u>must</u> be contained in the same replacement text. (Rule 29)

Proper Group/PE Nesting

Parameter-entity replacement text must be properly nested within parentheses.

For interoperability, if a parameter-entity reference appears in a *choice*, *seq*, or *Mixed* construct, its replacement text should <u>not</u> be empty. A connector (| or ,) should <u>not</u> be the first nor last non-blank character of the replacement text. (Rules 49, 50, and 51)

IV

Part

Required Attribute

When the default declaration is #REQUIRED, the attribute <u>must</u> be specified for <u>all</u> elements of the type in the attribute-list declaration. (Rules 52 and 60)

Root Element Type

The Name in the document type declaration <u>must</u> match the element type of the root element. (Rule 29)

Standalone Document Declaration

It <u>must</u> equal "no" if any external markup declarations contain a declaration of:

- An attribute with default values and the attribute elements appear without specifications for these attribute values.
- An entity (other than amp, lt, gt, apos, or quot) is referenced in the document.
- An attribute with values subject to normalization appears in the document with a value that can change as a result of normalization.
- An element type with element content and white space occurs directly within any instance of the element type. (Rule 32)

Unique Element Type Declaration

No element type may be declared more than once. (Rule 45)

Appendix E

XML Web Sites

New XML sites are being created every day. This selection is one based on mid-1999. The key three are the big two and Robin Cover's site, listed under individual Web sites.

Big Two Web Sites

World Wide Web Consortium is where the latest as well as the earlier versions of the XML Recommendations or Standards are located. This is the technical source for all XML.

http://www.w3.org/XML/

> **Note:** This book uses XML Recommendation 1.0 (10 February 1998) found at:
>
> **http://www.w3.org/TR/1998/REC-xml-19980210**

The Recommendation uses the Extended Backus-Naur Form (EBNF) notation for the XML formal grammar. To find out more information on EBNF, go to:

http://www.xml.com/xml/pub/98/10/guide5.html

The XML FAQ (Frequently Asked Questions) site is maintained by the W3C's XML Working Group. This is a quick way to get at some of the key issues or concerns with XML. It is found at:

http://www.ucc.ie/xml/

Web Sites of Organizations and Companies

See ArborText's site to find out about the ADEPT XML editor and other tools. ArborText is a pioneer in this area for SGML and XML.

http://www.arbortext.com

To learn more about document management systems and XML publishing, visit the site that belongs to Veo Systems, Inc.

http://www.veosystems.com

One of the areas in which XML is being used is push technology. For more details on this development area, see DataChannel's site:

http://www.datachannel.com

Some librarians and computer specialists have undertaken a project, Dublin Core, to devise a searchable language oriented towards documents.

http://www.uk.oln.ac.uk/metadata/resources/dc

To get more information about XML conferences, courses, and publications in general, the Graphics Communication Association's site is the place to go:

http://www.gca.org/conf/whatxml/files/whatisxml.htm

Microsoft has its own MSXML and parser. To find out the latest on Microsoft's view of XML, see its home page:

http://msdn.microsoft.com

To learn more about Virtual database (VDB) technology and how XML is involved, see Junglee's site:

http://www.junglee.com/tech/index.html

Note: Microsoft frequently revises its pages. If this URL does not work, just use the top page. Microsoft has many types of pages on XML; for example, to find out about the Extensible Stylesheet Language (XSL), do a search on XSL at

http://msdn.microsoft.com

The Platform for Internet Content Selection (PICS) is a project concerned with Web site content to control over user access:

http://www.w3.org/PICS/

Poet Software has developed an object-oriented database based on the principles of the Common Object Request Broker Association (CORBA) model as discussed in this book. The company is also involved in XML technology. The site includes white papers.

http://www.poet.com

For a tutorial on XML, see Architag University's site:

http://www.sgmlu.com

SoftQuad has developed Panorama Publisher and Panorama Viewer for multiple platforms. These tools support XML.

http://www.softquad.com

The Unicode Consortium's site has details on character sets, the Unicode Standard (Unicode 2.1).

http://charts.unicode.org/

A number of XML dialects have been developed. One of them is Chemical Markup Language (CML). For details on CML, check the site of Venus Internet of London, England.

http://www.venus.co.uk/

To look at information in the electronic commerce area, a site to go to is the one that belongs to webMethods. The company has an XML toolkit for data accessing, data handling, and data securing.

http://www.webmethods.com/

Note: webMethods has information also on Web Interface Definition Language (WIDL), which is important to object-oriented development. For a free download of the toolkit, go to:

http://www.webmethods.com/products/QueryView

IV

Part

The World Wide Web Consortium looks at a variety of, and perhaps all, forms of Web technology. One area is based on the idea that a Web resource can be represented as an object. This technology is Resource Description Framework (RDF). For details on RDF's grammar, tags, and attributes, see:

http://www.w3.org/TR/PR-rdf-syntax/

Yahoo has collected together a set of XML development links.

http://www.yahoo.com/computers_and_Internet/Information_and_ Documentation/Data_Formats/XML

Web Sites of Individuals

Tim Bray is a founding father of XML. He is one of the co-authors of XML Recommendation 1.0. He is also a programmer. He developed Lark, a Java-based XML processor, to validate the XML design requirements.

http://www.textuality.com/Lark/

James Clark is dedicated to the development of SGML and XML tools. Most of his work is free.

http://www.jclark.com/

Robin Cover, an expert on SGML and XML, maintains the most extensive resource site on these two areas by an individual. Besides having source materials, the site has many links.

http://www.oasis-open.org/cover/xml.html

Because XML is a subset of SGML, there may be reasons for understanding this markup language better. Look at Dianne Kennedy's SGML Resource Center:

http:// www.mcs.net/~dken/xml.htm

Other Sites Referenced in the Book

http://www.sun.com

http://www.w3.org/Style/**XSL**

http://www.w3.org/**DOM**

http://www.w3.org/**TR**

http://www.omg.org/corba/corbaiiop.htm

http://java.sun.com/docs/books/jls

http://www.ecma.ch/stand/**ECMA-262**.htm

http://www.rational.com/uml/index.jhtml

http://transactnet.com/products/toolkit/userguide/refman/widl/
    overview.html

Appendix F

XML Markup Examples

The first declaration is the XML declaration (Rules 23-26). It is to be used <u>only</u> if the document is well-formed, that is, the document adheres to the well-formedness constraints given in XML Recommendation 1.0. See Appendix D, "Constraints."

```
<?xml version="1.0"?>
```

The second declaration is the document type declaration (Rule 28), which can be followed by markup declaration(s) (Rule 29) and element declarations (Rule 45).

```
<!DOCTYPE Database [
<!ELEMENT Database (Author)* >
<!ELEMENT Author (Name, Title, pubdate, pages, ISBN, price) >
<!ELEMENT Name (LastName, FirstName) >
<!ELEMENT LastName (#PCDATA) >
<!ELEMENT FirstName (#PCDATA) >
<!ELEMENT Title (#PCDATA) >
<!ELEMENT pubdata (#PCDATA) >
<!ELEMENT pages (#PCDATA) >
<!ELEMENT ISBN (#PCDATA) >
<!ELEMENT price (#PCDATA) >
]>
<Database>
<!-- This is where the data goes (Comment, Rule 15) -->
</Database>
```

Example of nesting:

```
<para1> First level paragraph
<para2> Second level paragraph</para2>
</para1>

<para1> </para1> cannot be a content of <para2> </para2>.
```

Example of a comment:

```
<!-- Any comment goes here. -->
```

An example of a CDATA section where <greeting> and </greeting> are recognized as character data rather than as markup.

```
<![CDATA[<greeting>Hello from the Big D!</greeting>]]>
```

Example of an external declaration:

```
<?xml version="1.0"?>
<!DOCTYPE greeting SYSTEM "hello.dtd"
<greeting>Hello from the Big D</greeting>
```

The system identifier hello.dtd gives the URI of a DTD for the document.

Note: URI as used here is defined by Berners-Lee et al., a work in progress expected to update IETF RFC1738 and IETF RFC1808.

Example of an internal declaration:

```
<?xml version="1.0" encoding="UTF-8"?>
<!DOCTYPE greeting [
 <!ELEMENT greeting (#PCDATA)>
]>
<greeting>Hello from the Big D</greeting>
```

Example of a standalone document declaration:

```
<?xml version="1.0" standalone="yes"?>
```

Example of an xml:space declaration:

```
<!ATTLIST poem xml:space (default|preserve) 'preserve'>
```

Example of a simple xml:lang declaration:

```
xml:lang NMTOKEN #IMPLIED
```

Example of an xml:lang declaration with default values:

```
<!ATTLIST book xml:lang NMTOKEN 'grc'>
<!ATTLIST gloss xml:lang NMTOKEN 'de'>
<!ATTLIST note xml:lang NMTOKEN 'en'>
```

Example of a start-tag and end-tag:

```
<termdef id="dt-feline" term="cat">
</termdef>
```

Examples of element type declarations:

```
<!ELEMENT br EMPTY>

<!ELEMENT container ANY>

<!ELEMENT p (#PCDATA|emph)* >

<!ELEMENT %name.para; %content.para; >
```

Examples of element-content models:

```
<!ELEMENT div1 (head, (p | list | note)*, div2*)>

<!ELEMENT spec (front, body, back?)>

<!ELEMENT dictionary-body (%div.mix; | %dict.mix;)*>
```

Examples of mixed-content declarations:

```
<!ELEMENT p (#PCDATA|a|ul|b|i|em)*>

<!ELEMENT p (#PCDATA | %font; | %phrase; | %special; | %form;)* >

<!ELEMENT b (#PCDATA)>
```

Part IV

Examples of attribute-list declarations:

```
<!ATTLIST termdef
      id ID #REQUIRED
      name CDATA #IMPLIED>
<!ATTLIST list
      type (bullets|ordered|glossary) "ordered">
<!ATTLIST form
      method CDATA #FIXED "POST">
```

Example of conditional sections:

```
<!ENTITY %draft 'INCLUDE'>
<!ENTITY %final 'IGNORE'>

<![%draft;[
<!ELEMENT book (comments*, title, body, supplements?)>
]]>
<![%final;[
<!ELEMENT book (title, body, supplements?)>
]]>
```

Example of character and entity references:

```
Type <key>less-than</key> (&#x3C;) to save options.
This document was prepared on &docdate; and is
classified &security-level;.
```

Example of parameter-entity reference:

```
<!-- declare the parameter entity "ISOLat2"... -->
<!ENTITY %ISOLat2
      SYSTEM "hhtp://www.xml.com/iso/isolat2-xml.entities">
<!-- ... now reference it -->
%ISOLat2
```

Example of an internal entity declaration:

```
<!ENTITY Pub-Status "This is a pre-release of the specification">
```

Examples of external entity declarations:

```
<!ENTITY galley
    SYSTEM "http://www.myplace.com/template/Galley.xml">
<!ENTITY galley
    PUBLIC "-//Myplace//TEXT Standard galley template//EN"
    "http://www.myplace.com/template/Galley.xml">
<!ENTITY galley
    SYSTEM "../grafix/Galley.gif"
    NDATA gif>
```

Examples of encoding declarations:

```
<?xml encoding='UTF-8'?>
<?xml encoding='ISO-10646-UCS-2'?>
<?xml encoding='ISO-8859-1'?>
<?xml encoding="EUC-JP"?>
```

Example declarations:

```
<!ENTITY lt "&#38;#60;">
<!ENTITY gt "&#62;">
<!ENTITY amp "&#38;&#38;">
<!ENTITY apos "&#39;">
<!ENTITY quot "&#34;">
```

Index

About XML Authority

Product Overview

XML schemas enrich, illustrate, and validate information models for today's advanced Internet applications. XML schemas enable automated content creation and repurposing for both document and data intensive applications. XML Authority provides comprehensive support for the most advanced needs in schema development.

E-commerce and ERP applications utilize XML schemas to bridge business dialects and enable transaction automation between heterogeneous environments. Moreover, industry schemas document common vocabularies, enhancing collaboration and standardization. As native XML browsers become available, schemas will ensure the right information is made available to the right user.

XML Authority is a graphical design tool accelerating the creation and enhancing the management of schemas for XML. With support for data typing, solutions for data interchange, and document-oriented applications converge. XML Authority includes a toolset to help convert existing application and document structures to schemas, defining the basis for well-formed XML documents and enabling valid XML. With output supporting XML's existing and emerging schema standards, XML Authority provides adaptive qualities to XML deployments. XML Authority fully supports and extends the XML 1.0 specification for schema.

Comprehensive Schema Authoring and Management Environment

XML Authority's intuitive graphical interface provides comprehensive lifecycle management support of schemas for XML. Using XML Authority, schemas can be developed on a modular level and integrated for comprehensive solutions. Moreover, collaborative efforts for schema development are fully supported. This is especially useful when sharing schemas between organizations.

- Interactive graphical schema representation
- Schema Qlicker, point and click content model creation
- Real-time syntax checking, ensuring valid schema
- Concurrent cross referencing of schema design and source
- Tree view of document structure
- Workgroup support with versioning and change logging
- Audience-specific comments
- Assistants for getting started and improving results

Advanced Schema Development Support

XML Authority includes schema development support beyond the XML 1.0 DTD specifications, providing an incomparable toolset for advanced document publishing and data interchange applications. In addition to support for DTDs, XML Authority delivers advanced capabilities of the emerging DCD specification. Users of XML Authority enjoy the best of today's standards and the latest concepts in XML development.

- Reusable content model and attribute sets
- Data type support
- High fidelity round-tripping
- Robust parameter entity support
- Processing instructions, notations, and general entities

Schema Information Importing

XML Authority imports schema information residing in existing data structures and documents. Once imported into XML Authority, the schema can be modified and combined to create schemas for XML.

Diverse Output Formats

XML Authority outputs XML schemas and XML prototype documents. XML Authority outputs DCDs, DTDs, and XML schema. The output is formatted for easy legibility. The following schema syntax output formats are provided: DTD, XML-Data (IE-5 Compliant), XML Schema Definition Language (XSDL), SOX, DCD, DDML, and XML Exemplar.

The Companion CD

Through a special arrangement between Wordware Publishing and Extensibility, a 10-use trial version of XML Authority v1.0 is included on the companion CD-ROM. XML Authority is the most comprehensive tool available for the creation, conversion, and management of schema for XML.

To get started, simply open the HTML file titled Welcome to Extensibility on the CD. The CD also contains a helpful XML Authority Walkthrough designed to make you familiar with the software in less than 15 minutes and a complete XML glossary to help you become familiar with the language. For your reference, XML Authority includes detailed documentation to help you navigate through every feature of the software. For more information about XML Authority, please see the previous page.

The companion CD also includes a computer-based training course called Fundamentals of XML. It is based on the XML Recommendation 1.0 (10 February 1998). This requires a 640 x 480 high color (16-bit) monitor. To use Fundamentals of XML, either copy Xmlfd.exe to your hard drive and run, or double-click on Xmlfd.exe.

Caution: Opening the CD package makes this book nonreturnable.